A BLACK WOMAN DID THAT

BY
MALAIKA ADERO

ILLUSTRATED BY
CHANTÉ TIMOTHY

downtown  bookworks

ABOUT THE AUTHOR

MALAIKA ADERO, of Adero's Literary Tribe, LLC, works with writers and organizations developing and promoting books. She is the coauthor of *The Mother of Black Hollywood* with Jenifer Lewis (Amistad) and *Speak, So You Can Speak Again: The Life of Zora Neale Hurston* (Doubleday). And she is the editor of *Up South* (The New Press), an anthology of writings and photographs on the Great Migration. She calls New York City, Atlanta, and Knoxville home. **www.malaikaadero.com**.

Acknowledgments

Many thanks to the wonderful team who made this book possible: the Downtown Bookworks team, including Julie Merberg, Sarah Parvis, Georgia Rucker, Sara DiSalvo, and Samantha Guss. And a special thanks to Chanté Timothy for her beautiful images. You make magic!

ABOUT THE ILLUSTRATOR

CHANTÉ TIMOTHY (pronounced *Shan-Tay*) is an illustrator based in London, England. Her work is often described as bubbly, bright, and colorful. She's always dreamed of increasing representation in children's books.

downtown bookworks

Downtown Bookworks Inc.
265 Canal Street, New York, NY 10013
www.downtownbookworks.com

DEDICATION

**To the grandchildren and great-grandchildren
of Dorothy Lavern Crump Roebuck Bell**

"Language and how we use language determines how we act, and how we act then determines our lives and other people's lives."

— NTOZAKE SHANGE (born October 18, 1948, died October 27, 2018), poet, playwright, activist, and author

"DREAM THE WORLD AS IT OUGHT TO BE."

— TONI MORRISON (born February 18, 1931, died August 5, 2019), writer, editor, professor, and author

CONTENTS

Introduction	6
Jesmyn Ward	8
Stacey Abrams	12
Misty Copeland	16
Alice Coltrane	20
Madam C. J. Walker	23
Patricia Bath	26
Lorraine Hansberry	29
Mo'ne Davis	32
Harriet Tubman	35
Debbie Allen	38
Angela Davis	42
Meghan Markle	47
Barbara Harris	50
Ava DuVernay	54
Xenobia Bailey	58
Bethann Hardison	62
Alice Walker	66
Serena Williams	70
Coretta Scott King	74
Whoopi Goldberg	78
Hadiyah-Nicole Green	82

Amy Sherald	85
Mary Fields	89
Cathy Hughes	92
Mae Jemison	95
Nina Simone	98
Ida B. Wells	102
Zora Neale Hurston	106
Sister Rosetta Tharpe	110
Shirley Franklin	114
Oprah Winfrey	118
Shirley Chisholm	122
Bessie Coleman	126
Gwendolyn Brooks	129
Faith Ringgold	132
Michelle Obama	136
Glory Edim	139
Abbey Lincoln	142
Shonda Rhimes	146
Shirley Ann Jackson	149
Simone Biles	152
Ella Baker	156
Resources	160

INTRODUCTION

Boundary-breaking, bar-raising, world-changing . . .

There are millions of girls around the world who possess extraordinary beauty and spirit, accomplishing things we never imagined—and sometimes in the toughest of circumstances. Many come from families and communities without the means to encourage or support their hopes and dreams. History has recorded countless times when black women and girls made a way out of no way. Think of Harriet Tubman, an enslaved woman who liberated herself and hundreds of others and then helped the country win a war to end slavery.

What is it, that special thing we have? CaShawn Thompson called it our magic; she created the hashtag #BlackGirlsAreMagic and put the phrase on a T-shirt. Beverly Bond, a DJ and producer, came up with the phrase Black Girls Rock! as an "affirmation . . . that our young women need to hear today." She designed a T-shirt and an awards program broadcast on television to honor the black girls who rock. The concepts that these two individual women developed connected with masses of women and girls around the country and have grown into social movements.

One of my favorite things to do is to read the stories of magical black women. Knowing more about who they are and what they did with their superpowers helps me come up with ways to use my own passions and talents for good. The stories of women such as Toni Cade Bambara, Toni Morrison, Alice Walker, and others encouraged me in my pursuit of a career in book editing and writing. Debbie Allen inspired me to dance. Faith Ringgold, by her example, showed us all that we can be mothers *and* accomplished artists.

I've written this book, *A Black Woman Did That*, to show examples of what more than 40 black women did in their lives and with their work. I tell the stories of women who did more than people expected of them and more than they imagined for themselves—and others who, like Shirley Ann Jackson, took the advice of their parents and aimed for the stars. Mae Jemison traveled to space, Oprah Winfrey founded a television network, and Serena Williams remains at the top of her field in tennis, while running businesses, building schools in Africa and the Caribbean, and raising a daughter.

Each of these women was once a small girl looking for moments to utilize her magic to make a good life while being, in the words of writer Lorraine Hansberry, "young, gifted, and black." Shirley Franklin was inspired by Harriet Tubman, Coretta Scott King, and other activists to use her "sheer will to get something done." And, in Shonda Rhimes's words, "Whatever you can imagine is possible."

Who would have imagined that a black woman would receive a Nobel Prize in Literature? Toni Morrison did that. Who would have believed that a black woman would climb a flagpole like an elite athlete to tear down a Confederate flag at the South Carolina state capitol? Bree Newsome did that. Who would have known that a black woman would rank number one among the highest-earning female music stars? Rihanna did that. Every black woman and girl can **Do That**: live their dream and make their mark on the world.

—Malaika Adero

JESMYN WARD

Jesmyn Ward grew up on the Gulf Coast of Mississippi. Her family has been poor or working class and living in the same place for generations—in a part of the country with a particular reputation for oppressing African Americans. The state has historically ranked high in poverty and low in the quality of education it provides. Jesmyn was familiar with hardship as a young person in the 1980s and 1990s.

Years later, when she delivered the commencement speech at Tulane University in 2018, Jesmyn told the graduates about her grandmother, who worked in her father's fields as a child and had to leave school at 13 because in the 1940s there were no schools nearby that allowed African American students. She said, "My grandmother thought that if her children finished high school, they wouldn't have to work as hard as she did. She thought they wouldn't have to labor as housekeepers or as maids. But her kids' lives were as hard as hers." Many of Jesmyn's loved ones either "worked one dead-end job after another or were chronically unemployed." Her own mother cleaned houses for a living. Jesmyn was determined to have a better life. "So, I studied," she told the crowd.

For Jesmyn, schoolwork was not a burden, but classmates sometimes were. In public school, fellow black students picked on her for being a shy bookworm. Her mother's employer paid for her to go to a private school that had a better academic reputation. But as that school's sole black student, she was bullied and isolated by the wealthy white students because of her race and her background.

After graduation, she left Mississippi, traveling across the country to attend Stanford University in California. She says she wasn't academically "the standout student" that she'd been in high school, but she was determined to stick it out. And she did, earning a bachelor's degree in English in 1999 and a master's degree in media studies and communications a year later. She was drawn to literature and aspired to be a writer. But without a job, she moved back home to DeLisle, Mississippi. And six months later, tragedy struck Jesmyn's family. Her younger brother Joshua was killed when a drunk driver hit his car.

Jesmyn once hesitated to write about hurtful aspects of her past. But after her brother's death, her outlook changed. She felt driven to write about poor black people in Mississippi. "I didn't have a choice anymore," she has said. "I couldn't run from that desire to tell stories, that desire to tell stories about us and about the people I loved."

Encouraged by friends, she moved to New York City to work in publishing. She knew she'd rather be writing, but she also knew she had a lot to learn. "For two and a half years, I read," she said. "At the end of that time, I wrote and revised one short story." She kept writing and was accepted into a master of fine arts (MFA) program at the University of Michigan, where she studied creative writing and graduated in 2005.

Shortly after that, Hurricane Katrina devastated the Gulf region. Jesmyn was there when water rose up through the floor and filled her grandmother's home. Denied shelter by a white neighbor, she and her family waited out the storm in a truck parked in an open field. The trauma of the hurricane, of fighting against the elements for survival, changed her again. She eventually began to weave her experiences into the novel *Salvage the Bones*, which is about an impoverished family in the days leading up to the hurricane. In it, she vividly describes the hurricane's devastation: "She left us a dark Gulf and salt-burned land. She left us to learn to crawl. She left us to salvage."

HOME, SWEET DIFFICULT HOME

Jesmyn Ward returned to her birthplace of DeLisle, Mississippi, in 2010. In an essay in *Time* magazine, she attempted to explain why she decided to return to a place with such an ingrained history of racism. She wrote, "I remember that Mississippi is not only its ugliness, its treachery, its willful ignorance." It is also filled with memories of her family "flush with joy." In a 2017 interview, she said, "There's a feeling of belonging and of ease and of knowing who I am that I feel here that I don't feel anywhere else."

In spite of the brutal power of her writing, Jesmyn was met with rejection early on when she sent her work to publishers and agents. Often the rejections were not about how she wrote, but what she wrote about. She felt there was a subtext, or underlying message, in the responses she got from editors: "People will not read your work because these are not universal stories. I don't know whether some doorkeepers felt this way because I wrote about poor people or because I wrote about black people or because I wrote about Southerners." She kept on sending out her work, and ultimately her perseverance paid off. *Salvage the Bones* was not only published but it also won the prestigious National Book Award for Fiction in 2011. Two years later, she published a critically acclaimed memoir called *Men We Reaped*. In it, she recounts the stories of five young black men she knew—including her brother Joshua—who all died within four years of one another.

Jesmyn used her talent to express her pain, her joy, and the experiences of people who looked and sounded like the people she grew up with. And she has become one of the most celebrated young writers of her generation. In 2017, she became the first woman to receive two National Book Awards for Fiction when her novel *Sing, Unburied, Sing* won the award. In describing the book, the judges wrote that it was "a narrative so beautifully taut and heartbreakingly eloquent that it stops the breath." That same year, the MacArthur Foundation gave her a coveted fellowship (often referred to as a "genius grant"). Now wildly successful, she admits that she writes for her younger self. "She secretly dreamed of all this," she has said. "She wouldn't admit it, and she wasn't very confident about it, but she secretly hoped."

"I REALIZED THAT EDUCATION WASN'T ONE CHOICE. INSTEAD, IT WAS A LIFETIME'S UNDERTAKING."

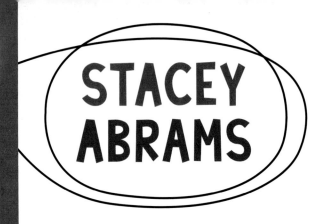

STACEY ABRAMS

Stacey Abrams is an introvert. As a young person, she says she had few close friends. When she played childhood games with her sister, though, she'd pretend to be "a tycoon, a superhero, or President of the World"—not what you'd think the ambitions of a shy girl would be. But to her parents, these goals weren't out of the question. They believed, not that she would actually be the "President of the World," but certainly that she could be anything she set her mind to.

Stacey's parents, Carolyn and Robert, had big dreams for each of their six children. They thought that the foundation for fulfilling those dreams was for the kids to "go to school, go to church, and take care of each other." They moved the family from Gulfport, Mississippi, to Atlanta, Georgia, so the whole family could take advantage of the many educational opportunities there. Carolyn and Robert earned their master's degrees from Emory University and became ministers in the United Methodist Church, while Stacey attended the best public school they could find in their Atlanta suburb.

After Stacey was chosen to be her high school class valedictorian, she was invited, along with other valedictorians from across Georgia, to be a guest of the governor at a reception in their honor. This was her first big step toward her dreams, but it was also her first reality check on what she'd have to overcome as a dynamic young African American woman. When she reached the governor's mansion, she was stopped from entering because a guard at the gate didn't believe she belonged there. Her parents kindly, but firmly, corrected the guard's assumption. But now, that crushing moment is the thing Stacey remembers most about the evening, not meeting the governor or being honored alongside her peers from around the state.

Being stereotyped set Stacey back a bit, but it did not stop her. She wrote in her book *Minority Leader: How to Build Your Future and Make Real Change* that she threw herself "into college life, hungry to become this new superwoman: the Breaker of Stereotypes, Destroyer of Black Woman Myths." And her choice of Spelman College, a prestigious historically black women's college, was the right place for her to be. There she found a supportive environment among girls who looked like her. And that gave her the confidence to go on to the LBJ School of Public Affairs at the University of Texas at Austin and to Yale Law School in Connecticut.

After law school, Stacey returned home to Georgia with stellar academic credentials. She practiced law, served as Atlanta's deputy city attorney, was active in Georgia's Democratic Party, and somehow found the time to write and publish novels, one after the other. The writing satisfied her creative side, but politics was her way of helping people, as her parents had taught her to do. Politics also became her vehicle for making history.

In 2010, Stacey became the first woman to lead a political party in Georgia—Democratic or Republican. She also became the first black person in the state house of representatives to become the house minority leader (that means she was the most powerful Democrat in the state house of representatives at the time).

The next challenge she took on was her biggest yet. Twenty-six years after she was stopped at the door of the governor's mansion, she launched a campaign to do what no black woman had done before— become a state governor. As a business owner and Yale-educated tax attorney, she was confident that she was the most qualified candidate for the office. "I am a civic leader," she said, "who helped register more than 200,000 Georgians." And she had a track record of leadership.

A WRITER TOO!

Stacey Abrams was an avid reader from a young age. In elementary school, she began reading chapter books before most of her classmates. She particularly loved science-fiction books. She started writing plays and stories in college. Then she moved on to writing the romantic suspense novels that led to publishing deals. She has published eight novels under the pen name Selena Montgomery.

In 2018, she fought a tough campaign, which earned her national attention. She became a star of the Democratic Party! It was a very close election, but her opponent, Brian Kemp, won. There was evidence that the election may not have been a fair one. While voters in heavily black, mostly Democratic districts had to travel great distances and wait in long lines to vote, hundreds of unused voting machines were discovered in a warehouse. Before the election, Kemp, who was Georgia's secretary of state, had ordered a review of the lists of people who could vote. It was later determined that 340,000 names had been improperly cut, making it impossible for those people to vote on election day. What's more, Kemp, Stacey's opponent, was overseeing the rules of his own election!

Stacey ultimately honored the system and acknowledged the results of the election, but was very clear in stating, "We cannot accept efforts to undermine our right to vote." And then she did something about it. She was so popular at this point that many people were urging her to run for a Senate seat or even for president in 2020. Instead, she launched an organization called Fair Fight to advocate for voter's rights all around the country. Among her most powerful supporters is former president Barack Obama, who said, "In a time when too many folks are focused simply on how to win an election, Stacey's somebody who cares about something more important: why we should. That's the kind of politics we should practice."

In little more than a decade, Stacey rose from being a force in state politics to a household name around the country. At the moment, her mission is "to advocate for free and fair elections . . . to ensure access to democracy for all." Her many loyal supporters would not be at all surprised if she ended up becoming president of the world after all.

> **"Not everyone's ambitions will be world domination or Carnegie Hall, but we should be driven beyond what we know and feel safe doing."**

MISTY COPELAND

Misty Copeland was seven years old when she found her first inspiration in movement. She was watching a Lifetime movie about gymnast Nadia Comaneci, who competed at the 1976 Olympic Games. Nadia made history for being the first in her sport to earn a score of a perfect 10. Misty was captivated by the grace and power demonstrated by a girl who was small like she was. She was especially impressed by Nadia's performance in the floor exercises, which appealed to her more than the tumbling and acrobatics of the other events.

Misty taught herself gymnastics, spending hours after school creating rhythmic routines. On the weekends, her backyard became her studio. "Whenever I danced, whenever I created, my mind was clear," she wrote in her memoir, *Life in Motion: An Unlikely Ballerina*. "I didn't think about how I slept on the floor because I didn't have a bed, when my mother's new boyfriend might become my next stepfather, or if we would be able to dig up enough quarters to buy food," she went on to explain.

Misty went through some trying times as a child. She was only two years old when her mother left her father and piled Misty and her siblings onto a Greyhound bus. They left Kansas City, Missouri, to move to the suburbs of Los Angeles. Misty's mother remarried. But while Misty's new stepfather was kind and a good provider, his alcoholism led to the end of the marriage. After the family left him, Misty wrote that she "would ride the bus and daydream about all the things a little girl should have that I didn't . . . problems no bigger than a pimple." Her mom worked odd jobs, trying to scrape together enough food to feed Misty and her six siblings. The family wound up living in a small motel room.

In middle school, she decided to try out for the drill team and was chosen as the captain. Being part of a group allowed her to make some friends and have more fun. It also gave her the opportunity to perform in front of audiences. The drill team coach, who had studied ballet as a kid, noticed how talented Misty was and thought Misty should give classical dance a try. She suggested to Misty that she to go to the San Pedro Boys and Girls Club and take the ballet class in their after-school program. Misty had never considered ballet before, but she respected her coach and didn't want to let her down. She checked it out. For more than two weeks, she watched the class in the gym, fearful that if she joined she'd make a fool of herself.

"I am a black woman, and my identity is not a card to play, or a label that I begrudgingly accept because it's been assigned to me. It's the African American culture that has raised me, that has shaped my body and my worldview."

The teacher had to coax her off the bleachers to join the class full of girls wearing leotards, tights, and slippers. Finally, she took her place at the barre. On her first day of ballet class, Misty wore a T-shirt, long gym shorts, and some old gym socks. She felt out of place. Everything about this kind of dancing—from the style of dress to the way the dancers moved—was new to Misty. "Most ballerinas start to dance when they are sipping juice boxes in preschool. I was 13 years old. Self-doubt taunted me," Misty recalled in her memoir. But she'd met a ballet teacher who would not let her give up. When fear crept in, she focused on looking, listening, and learning the techniques she was being taught. She began to see more dance, and she discovered new role models, including Debbie Allen (see page 38) and Paloma Herrera.

When she was 15 years old, Misty, who by then was recognized as a prodigy, was offered scholarships by five prestigious companies to attend their summer intensive programs. She chose to study with the San Francisco Ballet, both because it gave her the largest scholarship and because it was the closest to home. The next year, she chose to spend her summer with the American Ballet Theatre (ABT), where Paloma Herrera danced. Then, at 17 years old, Misty moved to New York City to participate in another summer intensive at ABT and then join their junior company.

A big city like New York can overwhelm anyone, and Misty was no different. But she also was energized by the city. It took a little while, but eventually she found a circle of support. Her mentors included actress Victoria Rowell, writer and ABT board member Susan Fales-Hill, and veteran ballerina Raven Wilkinson. They had her back when she joined ABT's main company. As a member of a company where her fellow dancers were both her friends and her competition, it was easy to feel lonely. But these women "became sounding boards and pillars I could lean on when it felt like too much," Misty wrote. She frequently talks about the importance of mentors in her life, but it was her discipline and artistry that resulted in her swift progress. By the time she was 19, she became a dancer in the corps de ballet of her dream company. Six years later, her performance of a pas de deux from *The Sleeping Beauty* led to her promotion to soloist at ABT—the first black soloist in the company in 20 years.

In 2012, Misty did something no black dancer had done before at ABT or any other major ballet company: she played the iconic title role in *The Firebird*. Sadly, shortly after her debut, she was forced to take five months off due to an injury. All of her hard work had taken a toll on her body. Since then, she has performed in many beloved ballets: *Don Quixote*, *Coppélia*, *Cinderella*, *La Bayadère*, *Swan Lake*, and more. In June 2015, this unlikely ballerina made headlines and history again. She was promoted, becoming the first black principal ballerina at ABT. At the time, Misty admitted to having doubts. She said, "I didn't know that there would be a future for an African American woman to make it to this level. At the same time, it made me so hungry to push through, to carry the next generation." With every performance, appearance, and advertisement that goes viral, she does just that.

STANDING OUT

A professional dancer's life can be lonely because of the long hours spent rehearsing and training. Misty Copeland's loneliness was magnified because she looked different. She was curvy in a way that is common to black girls but rarely accepted in the professional ballet world. When she was in the corps de ballet at ABT, Arthur Mitchell invited her to join his Dance Theater of Harlem. She was tempted to say yes. It would give her an opportunity to perform on world stages and place her in a company where she could stand out for her talent alone. Despite the downsides of choosing to be the rare black swan in a lake of white dancers at ABT, she became a star.

"IN LIFE, LIKE IN BALLET, YOU HAVE TO FIND YOUR BALANCE."

ALICE COLTRANE

Alice McLeod was playing the organ at Detroit's Mount Olive Baptist Church by the time she was nine years old. Later, she played percussion in her high school band. And sometimes she went along with her older half brother, Ernest Farrow, a saxophonist and bassist, when he hung out with musicians like saxophonist Joe Henderson and bassist Cecil McBee, whose stars were on the rise. As a young woman in Detroit, Alice formed her own band before traveling to Paris to study with jazz pianist Bud Powell. Over the decades, her deep interest in gospel, classical, and jazz gave her a strong musical foundation—one that allowed her to create a sound and style of playing of her own.

Early in her career, the scene was dominated by men, who often doubted a woman's ability to play at or above their level. But all it took to end that doubt was to hear Alice play. She quickly earned the respect of other musicians, who often jumped at the opportunity to perform with her. The greats in music came to love her, but none more than superstar composer and saxophonist John Coltrane.

Alice first heard John's music on the 1961 album *Africa/Brass*. "Before I even met him and became part of the group and part of his life," she said, "there was something in me that knew that there is a spiritual, musical connection, a divine connection, with this person." They first met when Alice was with a group led by vibraphonist Terry Gibbs. The group played a double bill with the John Coltrane Quartet at Birdland in New York City in the summer of 1963. John was impressed with Alice right away. Soon she replaced pianist McCoy Tyner in his band.

In 1965, Alice and John were married. The couple had three sons, John Jr., Ravi, and Oran, who were still small children when John

developed the illness that took his life. The year was 1967 and the world mourned with Alice, but it was she and her children who had to face life without John.

Alice found comfort in spirituality and music. Her first solo album, *A Monastic Trio*—with a sound that evoked gospel, jazz, new age, Indian, and African music—came out a year later. As time went on, her approach to jazz became more experimental and more spiritual. Interested in Eastern religious traditions, she released *Ptah, the El Daoud* (Ptah is the Egyptian god of creation, artists, and craftspeople) in 1970. Shortly after recording her next album, *Journey in Satchidananda*, she made a pilgrimage to India. "Hare Krishna" and "Sita Ram," two of the songs on her 1971 album *Universal Consciousness*, are based on traditional Hindu chants she learned there. By the time she passed away in 2007, Alice had recorded 20 albums as a bandleader—and made even more in collaboration with others. She played the harp on McCoy Tyner's album *Extensions* and collaborated with respected saxophonist Joe Henderson on his album *The Element*, playing the harp, piano, and other instruments.

Alice processed her grief with her artistry and committed herself to a spiritual practice of self-realization. She elevated the musical traditions of her African American upbringing, embraced world music and culture, and became one of the finest artists of her time.

IN THE NAME OF LOVE

Born Alice McLeod, she became Alice Coltrane when she married jazz legend John Coltrane. After spending some time in India, she chose a Sanskrit name as a part of her Hindu practice. She picked the name Turiyasangitananda, or Turiya, which she translated in English as "the transcendental Lord's highest song of bliss."

MADAM C. J. WALKER

Born in 1867, Sarah Breedlove lived a lifetime of experiences in her first two decades alone. She was an orphan by the age of seven, a wife by 14, a mother by 17, and a widow by 20. She had worked in the fields in Louisiana and Mississippi from the time she was a child. She lived in poverty then and through her marriage. But she was determined to have a better life. After her husband died, she and her daughter, A'Lelia, moved to St. Louis, Missouri, where three of her brothers had opened a barbershop. Upon arriving in St. Louis, Sarah began taking in laundry to earn around $1.50 a day. The work was stressful and was probably one of the reasons her hair began to fall out. In pursuit of a product that would regrow her hair, she found a path to prosperity.

At the St. Louis World's Fair in 1904, Sarah met a woman named Annie Turnbo, who had built a business making hair pomades. Because of stress, poor diets, and the use of harsh hair-care products, many black women like Sarah suffered hair loss. As a result, Annie's business was booming. She let it be known that she was looking to hire other women to sell her products. Sarah got on board, and what happened changed her life. She began cooking up oils and herbs on her own kitchen stove. A year after meeting Annie, Sarah relocated to Denver, Colorado. And a year after that, she married Charles Joseph Walker and began to call herself Madam C. J. Walker. She then launched a hair-care company of her own.

Looking back at her path, she said at the 1912 National Negro Business League Convention, "I am a woman who came from the cotton fields of the South. I was promoted from there to the washtub. . . . Then I was promoted to the cook kitchen, and from there I promoted myself into

The daughter of enslaved people, Madam C. J. Walker is considered to be the first American woman to be a self-made millionaire.

the business of manufacturing hair goods and preparations."

At the height of her business, she had bases in Indianapolis and in Harlem in New York City. Her sales force served clients from coast to coast and even abroad. When her daughter A'Lelia grew up, she joined the company. Both women grew rich but never forgot how they got there. Madam advertised her company and her products, like her Wonderful Scalp Ointment, in black newspapers and magazines, and she used her success to help thousands of women receive professional training in her beauty schools. Known as "Walker agents," her sales reps would sell her products door-to-door. Throughout her incredible career, she provided as many as 40,000 African American women with jobs.

Madam was generous with her time and money and provided great support to the anti-lynching movement led by Ida B. Wells (see page 102). In 1917, she and a group of influential Harlem men traveled to Washington, DC, to urge President Woodrow Wilson to make lynching a federal crime. (When the president refused to see them, they met with individual senators and representatives instead.) She contributed tens of thousands of dollars and resources to many people and causes, such as housing for the elderly and scholarships for students. During her life, Madam was one of the biggest contributors to the National Association for the Advancement of Colored People (NAACP). She pioneered effective marketing tactics, built a thriving business empire, and was the first person to employ large numbers of black women in business. And she was a great motivator. "Don't sit down and wait for the opportunities to come," she'd say. "You have to get up and make them!"

A'LELIA WALKER, THE JOY GODDESS

After her mother passed away in 1919, A'Lelia Walker continued to run the family business. She also maintained the mansion her mother built outside New York City. Designed by African American architect Vertner Tandy, it was named Villa Lewaro, and the Walker family opened it up to host cultural, political, and social events. Some of black America's leading figures—artists, scholars, politicians—and plain old partygoers visited the home and helped secure A'Lelia's reputation as the first major African American socialite. The poet Langston Hughes even gave her a nickname, "the Joy Goddess," for her ability to throw unforgettable, glamorous parties.

PATRICIA BATH

Patricia Bath's interest in medicine was sparked when she learned about the renowned Dr. Albert Schweitzer, a European philosopher and physician who often appeared in the news because of work he did building and running a hospital in Gabon in Africa. The story of his helping people with leprosy inspired her to take her first step toward a career in medicine. At 16, she applied for—and won!—a scholarship from the National Science Foundation to attend a summer program at Yeshiva University. There she studied the relationship between stress, nutrition, and cancer.

After completing high school in only two and a half years, Patricia went on to study chemistry and physics at Hunter College. In 1968, she got her medical degree at Howard University College of Medicine. She had a special interest in ophthalmology, which is the branch of medicine that deals with the structure of the eye and eye disorders and their treatment.

While getting her medical degree, she worked at two hospitals in different areas of New York City. This allowed her to see differences in the medical needs—and treatment options—found in different communities. She noticed that half of the patients she saw in Harlem—mostly black and brown—coming into the ophthalmology department were visually impaired or blind. At Columbia University, which served a mostly white community, far fewer people suffered from visual impairment. She wondered why. There must have been a reason for the disparity in people's eye health.

Patricia did what any good scientist would do. She dove into research on the subject and learned that

> **"When I encountered discrimination, I stayed focused on my goal."**

black people suffered blindness at twice the rate of white people. She concluded that lack of access to eye care was the reason for the higher rate of blindness. Patricia was disturbed. She regarded eyesight as a basic human right. Her solution was to propose a new worldwide system known as community ophthalmology, in which eye care volunteers were trained to test the vision of people in underserved communities and screen them for cataracts, glaucoma, and other serious eye conditions. As a result of her efforts, thousands of people who would have otherwise gone undiagnosed and untreated got the care that they needed.

"I hope that through my past legacy and future advocacy, the current and future generations of young scientists will not experience the hurtful wounds of discrimination of any kind."

In 1974, the native New Yorker moved to Los Angeles, where she became the first African American woman surgeon at the UCLA Medical Center, as well as the first woman to join the faculty of the UCLA Stein Eye Institute. Along with Alfred Cannon and Aaron Ifekwunigwe, she founded the American Institute for the Prevention of Blindness in 1976. In the middle of one cold, rainy night a few years later, she was working in the lab when she had a breakthrough using lasers to treat cataracts in the eye. (Cataracts can cause blurry vision and, if left untreated, they can cause blindness.) Patricia was thrilled by her findings. But not all of her colleagues, who were white men, were encouraging. She recalls telling the director of the lab about her breakthrough only to be met with disbelief. He said it was "impossible" that she had devised the treatment by herself. Some of her colleagues resented her success. In 1986, Patricia pursued her interest in laser technology at prestigious institutes in Berlin, Paris, and the town of Loughborough in the United Kingdom, where she developed a laser instrument to remove cataracts. More than 25 million Americans are affected by cataracts. Her invention, called the Laserphaco Probe, was patented in May 1988 and has since been used to restore the sight of countless people around the world. Some of the people she helped had been blind for decades. By 2001, having changed the state of medical care for African Americans and the state of eye care for people throughout the world, Patricia was inducted into the International Women in Medicine Hall of Fame.

LORRAINE HANSBERRY

Lorraine Hansberry's mom gave birth to her in the 1930s in the first black-owned and black-operated hospital in the nation. Her parents owned the building where they lived in Chicago and rented out the units they didn't use for themselves. Owning property meant that they lived better than most families around them. Lorraine loved her neighbors and had a joyful childhood. In a piece called "Chicago: Southside Summers" (originally published as "On Summer"), she wrote, "My childhood South Side summers were the ordinary city kind, full of the street games which other rememberers have turned into fine ballets these days, and rhymes that anticipated what some people insist on calling modern poetry." She described nights "spent mainly on the back porches where screen doors slammed in the darkness with those really special summertime sounds." She loved the company of the children around her but was sensitive to the fact that many of them lacked adequate shelter, clothing, and food. They were aware as well that she was better off than they were, with a father who was a landlord and worked in real estate.

Lorraine's father had his own struggles, though. Being a black man in a time when racism was practiced so openly—in the North *and* the South—meant that he had to work twice as hard as white businessmen to be successful. Housing in Chicago was racially segregated. There were many neighborhoods where black people were not welcome. When her father insisted on buying a home in one of these neighborhoods, he knew he'd have to fight in court and with the white neighbors to keep it.

When Lorraine was seven years old and her father moved their family into a white neighborhood, she, her mom, and her siblings were "spat at, cursed, and pummeled in the daily trek to and from school." But she thrived at Englewood High School and added theater to her interests.

She went on to the University of Wisconsin and the New School for Social Research, in New York City, but did not get a degree. She then studied art in Chicago and Mexico. She had a curious mind and a strong desire to express herself in words.

Lorraine was also interested in politics. She ultimately found the political and creative mentors she was looking for in New York City, where she moved in 1950. She joined a community of progressive and left-leaning thinkers. Shortly after arriving in the city, her first published work appeared in a magazine called *Masses & Mainstream*. She wrote for *Freedom*, a progressive, anti-racist newspaper founded by activist and performing artist Paul Robeson and edited by Louis Burnham.

"Though it be a thrilling and marvelous thing to be merely young and gifted in such times, it is doubly so—doubly dynamic—to be young, gifted, and black."

To achieve her goal of publishing her books, Lorraine had to get past the gatekeepers at publishing houses who doubted that stories, books, and plays representing black points of view could be popular and criticized her for not telling stories that all people could relate to. She disagreed. "I believe," she said, "to create the universal, you must pay very great attention to the specific." She wrote about the lives of the people she grew up with on the South Side of Chicago: her father and her father's tenants. As Imani Perry wrote in the biography *Looking for Lorraine*, Lorraine's work exposed "the national lies of liberty and democracy."

Lorraine was a prolific writer who gained a reputation for being one of the greatest thinkers of her generation. Her 1959 play *A Raisin in the Sun* was the first play by a black woman to be produced on Broadway, New York City's theater district. It tells the story of a black family in Chicago, similar to the ones she grew up with. In the play, a grown-up son, Walter Lee, argues with his mother over what to do with the life insurance money she receives after her husband's death. When Mama decides to buy a house in a racially restricted white neighborhood, the drama unfolds.

Lorraine died way too young. Her life was cut short by illness when she was 34. But the plays and prose that were her body of work made her immortal in the hearts and minds of her generation and beyond.

MO'NE
DAVIS

Mo'ne Davis found her black girl magic on the sports fields and basketball courts of Philadelphia while hanging out with her older brother and cousins. She had such superb athletic skills that everybody wanted her on their team, and only the best and most confident ever wanted to compete against her.

In 2008, when Mo'ne was seven or eight years old, a program director at a local recreation center named Steve Bandura saw her play. He said she was "throwing this football in perfect spirals, effortless, and running these tough kids down and tackling them." Impressed, he invited her to come to his team's basketball practice. Steve described in a newspaper article how focused she was when they trained. Right away, he recognized her as a promising athlete.

Mo'ne says that playing with boys was intimidating at first. Many of them were physically bigger and stronger. But her love for the sport got her past her fear. By the time she was 10 years old, she excelled as a point guard in basketball; a pitcher, shortstop, and third baseman in baseball; and as a midfielder in soccer.

She came to the attention of the world in 2014 when, at 13 years old, she became the first African American girl to play in the Little League World Series. She was one of two girls who played in that tournament and was the first girl in Little League World Series history to pitch a shutout. Fans went wild—and

> **"When I joined an all-boys baseball team, my mom wasn't too happy. I proved to her (and to me) that I could do anything I set my mind to."**

LIFTING UP GIRLS, ONE SNEAKER AT A TIME

Mo'ne Davis has used her fame to support good causes and to learn about branding and business. In 2015, Mo'ne partnered with footwear company M4D3 (which stands for "Make a Difference Everyday") to design a sneaker line. Some of the profits from her sneaker sales were given to a Plan International USA program called Because I Am a Girl, which helped girls around the world gain access to education.

people around the world took notice. "It was bottom of the sixth. . . . I knew I had to throw a strike in order to end the game. And as soon as [the ball] left my hand I knew that from that day forward my life would never be the same," Mo'ne said. Right after the tournament, *Sports Illustrated* did something it had never done before: it put a Little League baseball player on its national cover. Below the photo of her pitching was the headline "Mo'ne: Remember Her Name."

Mo'ne's history-making athletic accomplishments led to more unexpected opportunities. She starred in a Chevrolet car commercial that was directed by Spike Lee. She recorded camera phone videos with music superstar Drake and met President Barack Obama. She also collaborated with writer Hilary Beard on a book about her life and her experiences making sports history at such a young age. It is called *Mo'ne Davis: Remember My Name*. The star student athlete became one of America's most famous and inspirational young women. Mo'ne has proudly shared in interviews: "A lot of girls have told me that because of me they play baseball or they play on an all-guy's team."

Mo'ne is far from her peak in athletics or in life. In 2019, she started school at Hampton University, an HBCU (historically black college or university) in Virginia, playing softball as a member of the Lady Pirates. Her fans can't wait to see what's next for her promising life and her powerful pitching arm.

"I THROW 70 MPH—THAT'S THROWING LIKE A GIRL."

HARRIET TUBMAN

Harriet Tubman was named Araminta Ross at her birth, which was some time between 1820 and 1822. Araminta, or Minty, never learned her exact birthday. Enslaved people weren't issued birth certificates. And they were prohibited from learning to read or write, so they were rarely able to keep written records or family histories. The enslaved were regarded as property no different in the eyes of the law than a horse, pig, or cow—or even a wagon or piece of silverware.

When Araminta was about five years old, she was hired out by her master to care for an infant that belonged to another white family. If the baby cried, the child's mother would hit Araminta as punishment. After a few years, she was hired out to check muskrat traps and work in the fields, doing hard labor like an adult. She loaded timber and split fence rails. She adapted to hard work but never to the cruelty and mistreatment in bondage. She was rebellious by nature. When she was a young teen, a white man threw a two-pound weight to stop a black man from running away but hit Harriet by mistake, cracking her skull and knocking her to the ground. For years after the injury, she suffered from terrible headaches and would fall asleep at random moments. Araminta, forever disabled by the assault, came to view her disability as a blessing in disguise. She began to have visions, which she understood to be messages from God showing her the way to freedom.

In 1849, she ran away to the North, using a network of trusted people and safe houses known as the Underground Railroad. By then, she had taken her mother's first name and added it to her married name—she was known as Harriet Tubman. Harriet joined the abolitionist movement to end slavery. Then she repeatedly risked her own liberty and journeyed back into the South to guide family members and others to freedom.

She passed through forests and swamps—the whole time, running away from men with guns and vicious hunting dogs. She returned to the South more than a dozen times, liberating 300 people. Speaking at a women's suffrage convention in 1896, Harriet said, "I was the conductor of the Underground Railroad for eight years, and I can say what most conductors can't say—I never ran my train off the track, and I never lost a passenger."

Harriet learned the countryside so well that when the Civil War broke out in 1861, she became a valued asset to the military. She joined the Union army, working with government troops against the Confederacy— the slave states that seceded from the Union—as a spy and scout. She would visit enslaved people on plantations and gather crucial information, such as the locations of Confederate troops or their supplies. Harriet also served as a nurse, using her knowledge of medicinal herbs and treatments to cure infections and illnesses. (Disease killed more soldiers during the Civil War than the actual fighting.)

A year and a half into the Civil War, President Abraham Lincoln issued the Emancipation Proclamation, abolishing slavery in states that seceded from the Union. He opened up the ranks of the military, allowing nearly 200,000 black men and women to join. But one tiny black woman became the most celebrated of freedom fighters, and that was Harriet Tubman.

AFTER THE WAR

Harriet Tubman made Auburn, New York, her home in 1859. A few years later, she married her second husband, Nelson Davis, who had been a soldier in the war. In Auburn, she took in all sorts of people in need. In 1886, she bought two additional houses across the street in order to help more people. Ten years later, she partnered with the AME Zion Church, which renamed the rest home the Harriet Tubman Home. In 1911, she moved in to receive care, and there she spent the last two years of her long and triumphant life.

"I have heard their groans and sighs and seen their tears, and I would give every drop of blood in my veins to free them."

DEBBIE ALLEN

Debbie Allen was born and raised in Texas. But Debbie will tell you that her mother raised her and her sister, Phylicia, as "children of the universe" and therefore they did not feel defined by the prejudice they faced in racially segregated Houston. Debbie's mother, Vivian Ayers Allen, was a Pulitzer Prize–nominated poet who believed in arts education. When her daughter showed a passion for classical dance, Vivian was ready to support her all the way. Debbie's parents even paid a former dancer from the Ballet Russes, an influential Russian ballet company, to teach her privately.

At eight years old, Debbie auditioned for the Houston Ballet Foundation and was turned away because of her race. Debbie tested the waters again a few years later, but the foundation rejected her for a second time. Then, after her parents separated, Debbie's mother decided to move the family to Mexico City for a while. Mexico City was the first place Debbie lived where she could eat a hamburger at a lunch counter without any trouble. It was also where she was accepted into her first dance company, the Ballet Nacional de Mexico. After two more years of training and performing on stage, Debbie went back to Houston and auditioned for the foundation again. And this time, in 1964, six years after her first audition, 14-year-old Debbie was accepted. She was the first black student at the Houston Ballet Foundation.

Debbie had leapt over one big obstacle, but she would face others. No amount of education or accomplishment can overcome prejudice in every situation, even when you are a powerhouse of a dancer like Debbie was. When she applied to the North Carolina School of the Arts, she was told her "body type" was the reason she was rejected. Her brown skin, curvy body, and curly hair didn't fit the look they were after.

For the rest of high school, she focused on her studies, and then she found a new path. Howard University in Washington, DC, in the late 1960s was a different, more racially inclusive world. And it offered her the best of what she needed: a strong academic experience and a vibrant personal experience, where she felt supported, inspired, and encouraged. Debbie chose to study drama at Howard.

After graduation, she took her talents to New York City. In a short amount of time, she was on Broadway! She was cast in the musical *Purlie*, based on *Purlie Victorious*, a play written by acting legend Ossie Davis, and *Raisin*, a musical adaptation of *A Raisin in the Sun* by Lorraine Hansberry (see page 29). She also played a lead role in the classic musical *West Side Story*. And George Faison, with whom she danced in *Purlie*, made her a principal dancer of his company, the George Faison Universal Dance Experience.

Neither dance nor theater could hold all that Debbie had to offer. Soon, she was making her mark in film and television. In 1980, she appeared in the movie *Fame*, and in 1981, she was in *Ragtime*, based on the novel by E. L. Doctorow. *Fame* was such a hit that it spun off

"One of the main things I try to connect young people to is: Who are you? What do you care about in this world? Why are you dancing? What are you dancing about? What do you care about? What makes you laugh? What makes you cry? That. That is the driving force, and that could be for anyone. If you're a banker, if you're a builder, what do you care about? Why are you doing it?"

into a television series where Debbie reprised her character as "tough love" teacher Lydia Grant at a school for performing arts. She became a choreographer for the TV show, which ran for six years and received four Golden Globe Awards (including one for Debbie for best performance in a comedy or musical TV show!). She also directed episodes of the show and served as a producer for six episodes.

An amazing dancer, actor, and choreographer, Debbie has made unmatched contributions to American culture as a performing artist, but her greatest continuing accomplishments are as a producer and director. Directing single TV episodes led to full-time directing jobs. She directed more than 80 episodes of *A Different World*, a show that took place at a historically black college. She brought her perspective as a black woman to the stories of the students at the fictional Hillman College. Not only was it a ground-breaking television hit, but the show also made going to school cool. "We tripled enrollment of historically black colleges," Debbie says.

Shonda Rhimes (see page 146), who brought Debbie in as a director (and then an actor and producer) on her own hit show *Grey's Anatomy*, said that Debbie "put people of color on television and displayed them in ways they hadn't been seen before. She told stories that hadn't been told before. She gave people opportunities who hadn't been given opportunities before." It was Debbie, Shonda says, who was the real force in opening doors for people of color, including her.

SIBLINGS WHO SHINE

Phylicia Rashad, Debbie's sister, also became one of the most influential American women in the arts. She is beloved for her work as an actor, singer, and stage director. She was the first black actress to win the Tony Award for Best Actress in a Play (for her work in the 2004 revival of *A Raisin in the Sun*). She's best known for playing Clair Huxtable on *The Cosby Show*.

ANGELA DAVIS

Angela Davis and her three siblings were raised by a mother who taught elementary school and a father who owned a gas station. They did well for themselves and their children. But life wasn't easy. The town they lived in, Birmingham, Alabama, earned the nickname "Bombingham," because of racial violence perpetrated by white supremacists and hate groups such as the Ku Klux Klan. The African American neighborhood where they lived was even known as "Dynamite Hill" because attacks were so common. "Some of my very earliest childhood memories are the sounds of dynamite exploding," she said in a speech. "Homes across the street from where I grew up were bombed when they were purchased by black people who were moving into a neighborhood that had been zoned for whites."

A white man named Robert Chambliss became known as "Dynamite Bob" for his role in the violence, including as many as 21 bombings in Birmingham. In 1963, he committed his most infamous act. Along with other KKK members, he bombed the 16th Street Baptist Church, killing four girls who were there for Sunday school. The girls were known to the Davis family. They all lived nearby. "Violence was very much the norm," Angela recalled. But black communities in the South were unable to depend on official law enforcement. So they organized themselves into militias to defend and protect their families. Angela's father was a member of one of these armed patrols.

Angela showed an ability to lead and a knack for organizing early on. While in high school, she

IN MEMORY

The four girls murdered in the 16th Street Baptist Church bombing on September 15, 1963, were Addie Mae Collins, Cynthia Wesley, Carole Rosamond Robertson, and Carol Denise McNair.

WANTED

BY THE FBI

ANGELA YVONNE DAVIS

organized her peers—black and white—into study groups to look at and discuss ways to fight racism. Local police would arrive to break up their gatherings, falsely accusing them of causing a disturbance. The young people were coming together across racial lines in peace, and their First Amendment right to peacefully assemble was being denied.

When Angela was 15, she participated in an exchange program that placed black children from the South with white families in the North so they could attend school. She ended up at Elisabeth Irwin High School in New York City, where, she says, "We read the *Communist Manifesto* and where we read Freud." She explained, "It was a high school that had been created by a number of teachers who had been blacklisted in the public school system because of their politics." After that, she studied French literature at Brandeis University in Massachusetts, spending her junior year in France at the prestigious university known as the Sorbonne. In her last year at Brandeis, she began to study philosophy, which led to a scholarship to a university in Frankfurt, Germany. She remained politically engaged while she was abroad, participating in demonstrations against the Vietnam War. Angela later completed her doctorate in philosophy.

Back home in the United States, Angela sought out others who shared what she called her "love for oppressed people." She joined the Communist Party and then the Black Panther Party. Both groups advocated for justice for those in society who suffered most—poor people and people of color. Communists believe that fields, factories, mines, and machinery should be owned by the public and regulated by the government. Under communism, the goal is to distribute the wealth and recources of a country in an equal way. Capitalists, on the other

"YOU HAVE TO ACT AS IF IT WERE POSSIBLE TO RADICALLY TRANSFORM THE WORLD. AND YOU HAVE TO DO IT ALL THE TIME."

hand, believe in private ownership and a more hands-off approach from government, with less regulation of business.

In 1969, Angela began teaching at the University of California, Los Angeles (UCLA). By all accounts, she was popular among her students, but after being accused of being a communist by an undercover FBI agent, she was fired. She went to court and got her job back (only to lose it again for using "inflammatory language"). She said later in interviews, "One of the things that really impressed me when I was on the streets and fighting for my job at UCLA, was that whenever I spoke to black people, whenever I spoke in the black community, very few people had hang-ups about communism." In fact, many rather assumed that if she was drawing criticism, there must be something good about it.

Police brutality and bias against African Americans in the courts of law were, like now, a big problem in the 1960s, and that became the focus of Angela's social justice work. Outspoken people of color, such as a young man named George Jackson, were especially targeted. They became political prisoners. Jackson had been sentenced to one year to life in prison after being accused of stealing $70 from a gas station. Rather than just do his time quietly, he continued to speak out against injustice. He was then accused of another crime: killing a prison guard during a riot. Angela got involved with his case. She worked with his family, particularly with his brother Jonathan, who was also an activist. On August 7, 1970, Jonathan showed up in a California courtroom with guns, demanding the release of his brother. He and three others were killed when shots were exchanged with police as he attempted to leave the courtroom with hostages.

Angela was not in the courtroom, but guns used by Jonathan were registered in her name, so she was charged with crimes herself. She went into hiding and was placed on the FBI's list of "Ten Most Wanted Fugitives." She herself became a political prisoner upon her arrest. Her family, including her sister Fania, launched a campaign to ensure justice for Angela. "Free Angela" was printed on buttons and posters that were worn and posted all over by her supporters in and out of the black community and indeed all over the world. Now famous for her bravery, she became a powerful symbol of black pride. She sported the kind of huge, perfectly formed afro hairdo and wore the miniskirts that were the style of the day. Her striking appearance made her look like the revolutionary she was. Finally, after nearly 20 months of struggle, the courts found her not guilty of any crime. The campaign to set her free was a victory.

Later that year, she spoke on a California college campus for the first time since was fired from one in 1970. She said, "The major problem we are confronting today . . . is the problem of racism. . . . Black and brown and Asian and Native American people have always been the first victims of oppression and repression in this country. But I think that white people in this country, particularly white working people, should begin to understand that they too are exploited, and they too can be victims of repression."

Angela returned to teaching and writing, publishing books and papers, and continuing her activism. She remains a sought-after speaker and was named an honorary co-chair of the Women's March on Washington after the inauguration of President Donald Trump in 2017. She said from the stage during that event: "At this very challenging moment in our history, let us remind ourselves that we, the hundreds of thousands, the millions of women, trans people, men, and youth who are here at the Women's March, we represent the powerful forces of change that are determined to prevent the dying cultures of racism and hetero-patriarchy from rising again. We recognize that we are collective agents of history and that history cannot be deleted like Web pages." She remains a champion of the rights of the oppressed and continues to fight for the well-being of all people.

MEET EISA DAVIS

Filmmaker Shola Lynch directed a documentary called *Free Angela and All Political Prisoners*, released in 2013. Angela Davis's niece Eisa Davis, the daughter of her sister Fania, plays Angela in reenactments in the documentary, when footage was not available. Eisa, who is also an activist, has appeared on Broadway in *Passing Strange* and on the Netflix series *House of Cards*.

MEGHAN MARKLE

Meghan Markle comes from a mixed race family in Los Angeles.
When she was little, the neighbors repeatedly mistook her mom for a
nanny. "There was my mom," said Meghan in an interview, "caramel in
complexion, with her light-skinned baby in tow, being asked where
my mother was."

In the early 1980s, when Meghan was a child, interracial marriages
were uncommon—they had only been legal nationwide in America since
1967. Meghan had dark, curly hair and ivory skin, and people were always
asking her, "What are you?" Often she did not know how to answer the
question. Once, in the seventh grade, she had trouble figuring out which
box to check on a form she had to fill out in school. Should she pick
white? Or black? How could she choose one side of herself over the
other? Her father suggested she create her own box.

Meghan's parents divorced when she was six years old. Meghan
lived with her mother, but she continued to have a close relationship with
her father, who would often take her with him to his job. He worked in film
and television as a lighting designer and cinematographer (the person
responsible for the look, lighting, and framing of every shot being filmed),
so Meghan got to spend a lot of time on set as a kid. Her early exposure
to the film industry inspired her to pursue a career in acting.

After earning a degree from Northwestern University, Meghan began
acting professionally. But she admits that she had a tough time earning
roles. "I wasn't black enough for the black roles, and I wasn't white
enough for the white ones," she said, "leaving me somewhere in the
middle as the ethnic chameleon who couldn't book a job." She played a
nurse on a soap opera, landed a bit part in a film starring Ashton Kutcher,
and modeled on the game show *Deal or No Deal*. Then, in 2010, she

finally had her big break. She was cast as Rachel Zane on a hit TV show called *Suits*, which aired the next year.

She worked on *Suits* for more than seven years, but six years in, something unexpected happened. She met and fell in love with Prince Harry, the man who is sixth in line for the British throne. Meghan and Harry's 2018 wedding was one of the most watched televised events on the planet, with more than 29 million viewers in the United States alone. It was also, arguably, one of the most surprising. Though an interracial marriage was nothing shocking for Meghan, there was not a single branch of the royal family of England that had included a person of color. The feminist black American actress likely didn't imagine that she would marry into royalty—or that she would have to give up her career to be with the person she loved. But she did both.

While Meghan no longer works in Hollywood, she has expanded her platform to an international stage. She is committed to championing the causes that matter most to her, including women's rights. And the answer to the question "What are you?" now includes the Duchess of Sussex, a title given to Meghan by her grandmother-in-law, Queen Elizabeth.

PROUD FEMINIST

Meghan Markle has used her celebrity to champion causes like gender equality and social justice. In 2014, she started a lifestyle website called The Tig, where she wrote about food and fashion—and feminism. In a 2015 speech delivered before an assembly at the United Nations, Meghan declared, "I am proud to be a woman and a feminist. . . . It isn't enough to simply talk about equality—one must believe in it, and it isn't enough to simply believe in it, one must work at it."

She had been standing up for women's equality since she was 11 years old. As a young child, she wrote a series of letters of complaint about a sexist TV commercial for dishwashing liquid that suggested that only women washed dishes. In addition to writing to Procter & Gamble, the manufacturer of the soap, she wrote to Linda Ellerbee, host of a news program on Nickelodeon. Ellerbee had her on the show, and eventually Procter & Gamble changed the ad. At age 11, Meghan understood the power of her voice.

BARBARA HARRIS

Serving as pastor, priest, or rabbi has long been an honored tradition in the history of world religions—if you are a man. Women have only recently been welcomed into positions of power in faith-based organizations and, even now, their presence is rare. Barbara Harris is one of the few women who chose to pursue a life and career in the church, even though nearly all the leaders of her faith at the time were men.

She was always drawn to the church. In addition to her deep faith in God, she had a gift for communicating that was obvious even at a young age. As early as high school, Barbara wrote a column called "High School Notes by Bobbie" that ran in the Philadelphia edition of the *Pittsburgh Courier*, an established black-owned newspaper with a nationwide following. As a teenager, Barbara formed a youth group at St. Barnabas Church in Philadelphia that later became one of the largest youth groups in the city. She went to the Philadelphia High School for Girls, one of the best in the city, but found it more difficult than she'd anticipated. And worse than that, her teachers were unsupportive. The school's vice principal went so far as to say that Barbara and her other African American friends weren't smart enough to be there. Barbara wanted to leave the school after a while, but her mother made her stick it out. Later in life, Barbara said she was happy she did. The experience taught her—contrary to what her teachers had said—that she was smart and strong and that she could make it through adversity. "I learned that you can make it through tough situations," she has said, "that you don't let situations or people deter you from pressing forward."

After high school, she got a job with a black-owned public relations firm called Joseph V. Baker Associates, Inc. and took classes at the Charles Morris Price School of Advertising and Journalism at night. Her

work at the PR firm was consistently good. Over the years, she climbed the ladder at the company until she became its president in 1958. But Barbara wanted more than just success at work. She found a church community that suited her desire to grow spiritually and make the world a better place: the Church of the Advocate. It was both a church and a center of civil rights activity—a place where she could practice her faith and do social justice work with fellow churchgoers.

In 1965, Barbara led a church group to Montgomery, Alabama, to participate in the last leg of the now-famous march from Selma to Montgomery, led by Martin Luther King Jr. About that exceptional historical moment, Barbara said she felt like she "was supporting some people who had taken their life into their own hands and said it's going to be different. And walking with that great throng of people . . . it just felt good."

Her church hosted events that weren't welcome elsewhere in the city, including political education classes with the Black Panther Party and the 1968 National Conference of Black Power with the Black People's Unity Movement, which was attended by 2,000 people.

Barbara was among the first generation of African Americans working in the predominantly white corporate world. As a community relations consultant for the Sun Oil Company (later Sunoco), she showed her colleagues how they could give back to the communities who bought their products. At the same time, she continued her religious education. Many seminaries that trained clergy did not accept women. And Barbara did not want to give up her job just yet. So instead of attending a seminary full-time, she took religion courses at various schools, including Villanova University and the Pennsylvania Foundation for Pastoral Counseling.

"THIS WAS NOT A SMOOTH JOURNEY, BUT A JOURNEY CERTAINLY WORTH TAKING."

Joining the ministry was what she felt she was put on earth to do—her true vocation. And the church was slowly changing the rules. Finally, in 1976, the Episcopal Church recognized that women could be priests. But many church leaders and followers resisted. They were just not ready to accept women in positions of power. Some churches only allowed female priests to work as assistants or assigned them to smaller churches. Barbara's mother disapproved, and her friends were skeptical at first. But Barbara persisted, and in 1979, she was ordained a deacon in the Episcopal Church.

The following year, she moved up in the church hierarchy. She became a priest and began serving the community at St. Augustine of Hippo Church in Norristown, Pennsylvania. She remained there until 1984. She combined her background in journalism with her church work and became the executive director of the Episcopal Church Publishing Company, publisher of *The Witness*, a magazine that championed social justice causes. Barbara brought her voice to the magazine. She said, "In my column, I wrote mostly about the struggle for civil liberties for blacks and other minorities." She also became chaplain to the Philadelphia County Prison.

Barbara was elected to be the bishop suffragan (a member of the clergy who helps the bishop above her) of the Diocese of Massachusetts in 1988, but was met with the objections of many who looked at her background and thought that her advocating for peace, gay rights, women's rights, prisoner's rights, and the environment made her too radical. They also pointed to her lack of formal seminary training. Barbara did not waver. And in 1989, she was ordained, becoming the first woman to serve as a bishop in the Anglican Church. The accomplishment made history, but she also faced a lot of opposition because, as she says, "I was a woman. I was black. I was divorced . . . I was outspoken." When asked how she got through the backlash, she explained, "There were enough people supportive and confident in my ability to exercise this office and enough people praying for me," including her mother, who had changed her opinion about women being clergy and cheered her daughter on. During her next 13 years of service, Barbara changed the minds of many reluctant people, who now admire her work and sing her praises.

AVA DUVERNAY

Ava DuVernay was a California girl who spent her summers in Alabama. She lived with her mom and stepdad in Lynwood, just outside of Compton—a Los Angeles neighborhood known for its hip-hop and gang culture. She was surrounded there by a loving family that included an aunt who, in Ava's words, was "a ferocious movie watcher and fan with an encyclopedic knowledge of film." This aunt inspired Ava in her appreciation of art and film.

Ava describes herself as nerdy. Rather than hanging out with the cool girls, she liked to spend her lunchtime working in the school office. She credits her strong work ethic to her stepfather. She grew up watching him joyfully going to work at his own business installing flooring. He said to her, "If you can find work that you love, you'll never work." His wise words stuck with her. She found her first job as a teenager, working in a frozen yogurt shop. When she served customers, making "the perfect spiral" of yogurt was a point of pride.

Film was not on her radar in college. She earned a double major in English literature and African American studies at the University of California, Los Angeles (UCLA). She initially hoped to pursue a career in journalism. She landed an internship at CBS News, but didn't enjoy it as much as she imagined, and her enthusiasm for the field faded. "I worked at FOX and a couple of big PR firms for about four years. Was good at it," she said. She had ideas, though, about how public relations and publicity could be done better, especially where projects involving young people and black people were concerned. So, in 1999, she started her own agency. Clients hired the DuVernay Agency (DVAPR) to promote TV shows and films, including hits like *Spy Kids*, *Shrek 2*, and *Dreamgirls*. One day while working, she found herself on a movie shoot near where she grew up. A light bulb went on in her head, and she thought, "I could be making this film." She had her own ideas, her own vision, her own stories to tell.

Ava picked up a camera when she was 32 years old and began to make films independently while running the agency. *I Will Follow* was released in theaters in 2011, and film critic Roger Ebert called it "one of the best films I've seen about the loss of a loved one." Ava brought her stellar skills as a publicity and marketing person to her creative work as a filmmaker, particularly with her next feature film, the critically acclaimed *Middle of Nowhere*.

Ava was emerging as a filmmaker and wanted to bring her peers along with her. So she founded Array (previously the African-American Film Festival Releasing Movement), a collaborative of what she calls "like-minded black arts organizations around the country that come together to distribute black films [to movie theaters]."

The film that put her on the map was *Selma*, released in 2014. In it, David Oyelowo (who also starred in *Middle of Nowhere*) portrayed Martin Luther King Jr. during a civil rights campaign to help register voters in Alabama. It received Golden Globe and Academy Award nominations for Best Picture. It was the first time a film directed by an African American woman was up for these awards. Ava herself won a Best Woman Director award, given by the Alliance of Women Film Journalists, and was named Best Director by the African-American Film Critics Association.

In early 2016, Ava was busy working on *Queen Sugar*, a TV show she created and produced, based on a novel by Natalie Baszile, about three African American siblings who inherit their father's sugar farm in Louisiana, when she got an email from a Disney executive. In it, she was offered a job directing *A Wrinkle in Time*, based on a beloved

LEARNING BY READING

Ava DuVernay wrote the screenplays for both *I Will Follow* and *Middle of Nowhere*. She says she learned how to write scripts by reading them. "A big part of writing is reading," she said. "I had read almost every screenplay of all the 100 films and TV episodes" that she worked on as a publicist early in her career. She came to understand how a script is put together by studying them.

fantasy novel of the same name by Madeleine L'Engle. It is an exciting tale about a girl who travels across the universe with her little brother and her friend and saves the world. When she took on the project, she became the first black woman to direct a film with a budget of more than $100 million.

The projects Ava chooses often bring attention and add insight to issues of social justice. Her 2016 documentary *13th* (the title refers to the Thirteenth Amendment to the Constitution) draws a line connecting slavery, Jim Crow laws, and the mass incarceration of black men in America. She cowrote and directed the four-part dramatic series *When They See Us*, which tells the story of five black boys who spent years in prison for a terrible crime they did not commit. The case unfolded during the spring of 1989, and the young men became widely known as the Central Park Five. But Ava didn't use that moniker in the miniseries, believing that it dehumanized the falsely accused young men, Yusef Salaam, Kevin Richardson, Antron McCray, Raymond Santana Jr., and Korey Wise. The powerful miniseries, released in 2019, renewed public outrage about the injustice and revived people's commitment to fixing long-broken parts of the US justice system.

> **"I want more girls to be able to see themselves behind the camera creating images we all enjoy, and I want to call attention to the fact that women directors are here all over the world."**

Ava is not new to combining her artistic work with an effort to change the world, but she said that she once resisted being seen as the "social justice girl" in Hollywood. "But, as I've become older and, I think, more mature about it," she said, "I'm okay with being social justice girl." Great art has tremendous power to change the hearts and minds of people.

XENOBIA BAILEY

Before she was famous for being nationally recognized fiber artist and cultural activist Xenobia Bailey, she was Sherilyn, a child growing up in the predominately white city of Seattle, Washington. She described her coming of age as "very challenging for a creative black girl." She looked different from most of the people around her, and she was treated differently too. It left her feeling disregarded and lonely. School was particularly tough. "No matter how much work I did," she recalls, "even extra credit work, I always got Ds. I was held back in third grade."

In contrast, she was happy at home. Her mom brightened their house with tablecloths, curtains, and other housewares. She used old textiles and other materials she found that cost little or no money, long before the idea of upcycling was trendy. Xenobia described her mother's style as "a funky, chic urban household aesthetic that brings that beauty to a home." The friendly African American community where she lived gave her a sense of security, and the lush outdoor landscape of her hometown inspired her. She often says that she was first introduced to literature and art by nature. "Poetry was in the air," she has said.

"I first knew I was an artist when I was about nine years old," Xenobia said. "One day I drew this bike. We had a parent-teacher's day, and my mother came to the school. My teacher took her to the side and showed her this bike that I drew. And my mother got me a bike after that. So I thought there was some magic to this thing."

Xenobia didn't blossom as a student until college. At the University of Washington, she discovered ethnomusicology, the study of music and its relationship to culture, and she said, "the whole world opened up to me." She then went across the country to pursue her education in New York City—with a little help from home. The Seattle chapter of the

> "I make art to stay sane. . . . It's a way of identifying or becoming visible and communicating without having to verbally communicate who I am and what I'm about."

Links, an African American women's social club and service organization, provided financial support to help her get to Pratt Institute in Brooklyn. But Xenobia had issues with the way art and design were taught there. She believed her teachers did not fully embrace or respect black culture and its impact on design. Nonetheless, she earned a fine arts degree from Pratt in 1977.

Xenobia was fascinated by how everyday objects are made both to be useful and to look beautiful. At school, while she was studying industrial design, she found that "it was hard designing for the mainstream," which was what her professors wanted her to do. She felt that her originality was being stifled. "Everybody has their own signature aesthetic, and mine is the aesthetic of funk," she explains. The concept "comes from the African American household—the way colors were used, the way that patterns were used together, and the way that textures were used together." Xenobia has said that her aesthetic is rooted in the way her mother (and probably her grandmother too) and the women in her community embraced and used colors and patterns.

She had great ideas, but she did not have the money to buy the expensive tools necessary to professionally carry out her plans. So she took another route. She learned to crochet from a fellow artist and found that she could apply her creativity to making beautiful and useful things that way. Plus, the tools she needed—a crochet needle and yarn—were affordable. Needlecraft allowed her to grow as an artist and designer and produce objects that people could use, like hats. She put her unique spin on the designs, and her hats were a big hit.

Now called Xenobia Bailey, she made a name for herself in more than one way. She went from making hats to clothing, all while developing her own unique style of mixing colors, creating patterns, and incorporating other objects such as beads and shells. Her work was featured in women's lifestyle and fashion magazines by fashion-forward editors. Then she moved beyond designing clothing and accessories to become a name in fine art circles, especially in Harlem, where she lived for many years. She works in a range of media, from crocheted mandalas, wearable art, tents, and soft sculpture to photography and furniture design. At the root of her art is a use of color that's like a language of her own.

Much of her art has been acquired by individual collections, galleries, and museums. But Xenobia has also been commissioned to create public art projects to be enjoyed by everyday people in everyday life. In New York City, she was chosen to design a mural in the Hudson Yards subway station. She titled the three-part, 2,788-square-foot mosaic mural *Funktional Vibrations*. To make it, she crocheted pieces, which were then photographed. Then she worked with local craftspeople, who used enlarged digital images of her work to create the mosaic tiles for the installation. The craftspeople matched her yarn colors and re-created the texture of woven materials in the glass tiles, which now cover parts of the ceiling and a large dome in the station.

Xenobia incorporated music into the piece as well. "The dome piece is just crocheted circles, mandalas, and squares, and they are embroidered together. Some of them have 45s on them," she said. (A 45 is a type of record, usually containing a single song.) "Two pieces are from the Atlantic record label. And the reason why I used the Atlantic label is because of the Atlantic slave trade that brought us here," she said. The artwork is also, she says, "the cosmos—the coming of life and the ending of life and everything in between." As subway riders pass through the station, they can look up and around and be taken for a moment into Xenobia's colorful cosmos. *Funktional Vibrations* is not her only large-scale public work. She continues to exhibit in museums around the US and in public spaces. She is currently working on the ceiling of the grand reading room at the Martin Luther King Jr. Memorial Library in Washington, DC.

"I believe in searching for breakthroughs when problems appear. There is a great deal of disappointment that comes with being an artist. But the victories and success snap all of the trials and tribulations together."

BETHANN HARDISON

Bethann Hardison's name is synonymous with high fashion.
Raised in Brooklyn, one of New York City's five boroughs, she attended
George Wingate High School in the predominantly white neighborhood
of Flatbush, a bus ride away from the black neighborhood of Bedford-
Stuyvesant where she lived. She was culturally outnumbered, but the
experience was "one of the best things that ever happened," she said,
giving her the confidence to excel in any kind of situation. She did well in
her classes, made friends, and got involved in extracurricular activities too.
She even became the school's first black cheerleader. After high school,
she attended New York University's art school, but she didn't do so well.
"I was so bad. I didn't know how to draw. I didn't know anything," she
said in an interview. She went on to study merchandising at the Fashion
Institute of Technology. While there, she got pregnant with her son. Her
mother and grandmother, in particular, helped Bethann raise him.

She didn't have set plans for her future, but Bethann was willing to
work hard. She took jobs at a telephone company and a hand-painted
button factory, and once even worked as a corrections officer at a prison.
At the time, she was 21 years old, guarding women who were the same
age as her. She has said, "I had to act tough . . . because [the inmates]
challenge you." After that, she found a job in Manhattan's Garment
District—the heart of America's fashion industry. She learned on the job
about how clothes were designed, constructed, and merchandised.

In the past, the fashion industry excluded black designers, but it
began to open up in the 1960s and 1970s. A young black designer
named Willi Smith saw Bethann around and thought she'd be a perfect
muse—the person who serves as a source of inspiration for an artist.
She agreed to work with Willi, and he created new designs with her in

mind. Soon others sought her out as a model. Bernie Ozer, a fashion buyer who had a huge influence over trends in the fashion industry, put her in a runway show. Bethann credits Bernie with putting her "on the map." Bernie loved the theater and showmanship, and he saw something special in Bethann. "I was theatrical," she said of her first show. "I didn't walk like the other girls—I performed a bit." She brought her background as a child tap dancer to her performance as a model. "When you tapped," she said in an interview, "you had to wow the crowd."

Bethann was hired as one of 10 black models to walk the runway in a show at the Palace of Versailles in France in 1973. The event began as a fundraiser to help restore the more than 300-year-old palace. But it became much more than a fashion show. It turned into a competition between American and French design houses. The French took great pride in being recognized as the leaders of the fashion world, so the stakes were extra high for the American designers. But they had a secret weapon: a group of models with a look and style of movement that Europe had never seen. This incredible group of models included Pat Cleveland, Norma Jean Darden, Alva Chinn, and, of course, Bethann Hardison. The brown-skinned beauties brought energy and excitement, prancing and dancing down the runway. In contrast, the European models had a straightforward, expressionless way of walking so they would not draw attention away from the clothes they wore. The Americans combined elegance with movement and emotion, making the clothes and the moment even more memorable. There were more than 500 people in the audience, and it was unlikely that most of them associated black people with high fashion. "I defied everybody in that entire audience,"

"TO NOT ACCEPT DIVERSITY HURTS EVERYONE. IT HURTS THE FASHION INDUSTRY. IT HURTS SOCIETY."

Bethann recalled. "I really let them know that we are here to take this because we have been put down so much." The black girls rocked, the American designers won the Battle of Versailles, and the show became the talk of the fashion world.

Bethann's look and personality took her to the top as a model from the late 1960s through the 1970s, but afterward she took a new career path. She became a fashion consultant and joined a startup modeling agency called Click, where she booked models, produced fashion shows, and helped grow the business. Then, she says, her friends convinced her to start her own company, Bethann Management. She launched the company in 1984. She nurtured the careers of young talent and seasoned models, including models of color who didn't fit a European ideal of beauty, including Veronica Webb and Tyson Beckford.

In 1988, Bethann co-founded the Black Girls Coalition to celebrate and provide advocacy and support to African American models. In the mid-1990s, when she noticed that models of color began to disappear from runways and magazines, her mission began to change. She used her influence in the industry to speak up about the rise in racial discrimination in fashion. She wrote letters to industry leaders, challenging them on their hiring practices. She brought together influential members of the fashion industry—writers, editors, agents, managers, and models like Iman—to hold a press conference and find ways to encourage positive change.

People credited Bethann's leadership style as a factor in the fashion industry's progress. Rather than accuse her fellow industry gatekeepers of being racist, she showed them how their business decisions could make a negative social impact. To the surprise of many, they not only responded with respect but also stunned her with awards, including the 2013 Frederick Douglass Award and the Council of Fashion Designers of America (CDFA) 2014 Founder's Award. At the CFDA Awards, she told the audience, "I'm not here to put anyone down. I'm here to bring everybody up."

Bethann's son is actor Kadeem Hardison. He famously played the character Dwayne Wayne on the hit television show *A Different World* from 1987 to 1993.

ALICE WALKER

"Three dollars cash for a pair of catalog shoes was what the midwife charged," Alice Walker wrote, about being born on a cotton farm in Eatonton, Georgia. Her parents were sharecroppers, and her mother later became a maid for the farmer's family. Together, they lived on the same land where they worked. The landowning farmer and his family lived in wealth on the same land where Alice, her seven siblings, and their parents lived in poverty. Sharecroppers cultivated and produced the landowner's crops but rarely reaped any profit.

The poverty that marked Alice's childhood was one thing, but the discrimination her family experienced because they were black was another. "I grew up in the South under segregation," Alice has said. "So, I know what terrorism feels like." She explained further: "When your father could be taken out in the middle of the night and lynched just because he didn't look like he was in an obeying frame of mind when a white person said something he must do. I mean, that's terrorism."

Alice's mother cleaned the farmer's house, but she also stood up to him, like she did to everybody else. Once, he came to their house and told Alice's mother that her children needed to be out in the fields picking his cotton and working his land. Alice says her mother defied him and replied, "These children are my children, and they are going to be educated." Instead of putting her children to work, she put them in school. Alice was enrolled in school when she was four years old.

The worst thing that happened to Alice as a child occurred when she was eight years old. While playing with her older brothers, she was injured in a BB gun accident that left her scarred and blind in one eye. Her self-esteem withered, and she retreated from other people. Ultimately, though, her injury led to a new passion: reading and writing.

Reading introduced her to new ideas and places, and writing was a way to express her feelings.

By the time she boarded a bus to Atlanta to attend Spelman College, an HBCU (historically black college or university), she knew what she wanted to do with her life. But something happened on the ride that gave her another life's work. The driver asked her to move from the front of the bus to the back, at the request of a white passenger. In that moment, Alice came to believe that she "would have to be politically active in order to achieve enough freedom to write." The white bus driver and the passenger could get away with racist behavior because they had a system of injustice behind them. She therefore needed to add social justice work to her vision for her life ahead.

MEET REBECCA

Alice Walker's daughter, Rebecca Walker, is a respected writer in her own right. Inspired by her life, Rebecca wrote *Adé: A Love Story*, the story of a biracial American girl finding love in Kenya, and *Black, White, and Jewish: Autobiography of a Shifting Self*.

After two and a half years at Spelman, she transferred to Sarah Lawrence College in New York, where she completed her undergraduate studies. She returned to her home state after graduation and joined efforts to register voters in districts where black political participation was being undermined. She also began to teach low-income children in a program called Head Start, which was backed by Congresswoman Shirley Chisholm (see page 122). The civil rights movement was at a high point, and Alice was an active participant in demonstrations and protests as she began to create a body of literature.

Alice was living in Mississippi when she wrote *The Third Life of Grange Copeland*, her 1970 novel about a sharecropper like her father, and began *Meridian*, her 1976 novel about a civil rights worker like herself. She brought her life experience and her political worldview to the craft of storytelling.

In the late 1960s, Alice added the women's movement to her scope as an activist, and she soon discovered that black women weren't well represented. She felt that the label "feminist" and the ideas associated with it didn't reflect the experience of black women, and she wrote about it in a 1983 collection of essays called *In Search of Our Mothers' Gardens*. She coined a new term, *womanist*, to apply to black women and women of color. A womanist, in her words, "loves music. Loves dance. Loves the moon. *Loves* the Spirit. Loves love and food and roundness." She wrote, "Womanist is to feminist as purple to lavender."

Alice's nonfiction work established her as a critical thinker and a feminist icon, but it is her fiction that touched people of all backgrounds and earned her the biggest audience and greatest commercial success. Her 1982 book, *The Color Purple*, tells the story of Celie, a shy young woman who is abused by her husband, Mister, until she learns more about herself, with the help of a few loving friends. The novel is told through letters that Celie writes to God, who she believes is the only one who listens to her, and to her beloved sister Nettie, a missionary in Africa, with whom she's lost contact. The book, both heartbreaking and inspiring, won a Pulitzer Prize, one of the greatest awards in literature.

FROM PAGE TO SCREEN AND STAGE

Music legend Quincy Jones was so moved by Alice Walker's novel *The Color Purple* that he jumped at the chance to produce the film version. He wrote the music and asked Steven Spielberg to direct the movie. Beloved actor Danny Glover and newcomers Whoopi Goldberg (see page 78) and Oprah Winfrey (see page 118) were cast in leading roles. *The Color Purple* is a classic American story, appreciated all over the world. It has even been turned into an award-winning Broadway musical.

"Part of what any writer does is try to help you see what it is they see. That's really all you can do. You can't make people change if they're not moved to do it, but that's why we have writers, poets, fighters, and dancers."

SERENA WILLIAMS

Serena Williams was part of her father's family business plan before she was even born in 1981. Richard Williams knew that sports champions brought home big cash prizes, so he and his wife Oracene studied tennis in order to teach the game to Serena and her older sister, Venus. He also moved the family from Long Beach to Compton, California, where they could use free public tennis courts to practice their serves and volleys, when the girls were young.

Serena has many siblings, but training with and competing against Venus made their bond special. Serena was her older sister's biggest fan from the beginning. She wanted to be just like her, so much so that if Venus wanted something, Serena wanted it too. "When we were younger," Serena has said, "It was difficult for me to play Venus because she'd always beat me so badly. I had to improve just so I could stay in the game." Serena had to grow into herself—and over time, she did just that. In 1999, when Serena was 17, she won the US Open, something Venus had yet to achieve. Over the course of the next 20 years, she would win the major tennis competitions known as the Grand Slam tournaments—the US Open, Australian Open, French Open, and Wimbledon— many times over. In fact, Serena has earned 23 Grand Slam titles, more than any other athlete, male or female, in the modern era of the game. With her strong serve, impressive speed, quick reactions, and signature backhand, she is a powerhouse on the court.

Although they love tennis, Serena and Venus have always had other interests too. "We get bored

> "If you want to be the best, you've got to emulate the best. . . . You have to hang around people, and you have to look at people who are the best."

quickly," Serena has said. Both sisters have always been aware that sports careers are short and that most professional athletes retire while they are still young. When their tennis careers end, neither Williams sister wants to have to wonder, "What should I do now?" So, in addition to their grueling training schedules, the sisters pursued other goals off the court. Venus studied fashion design and business administration. She has a clothing line called EleVen and an interior design company called V Starr Interiors. Serena spent two years studying at the Art Institute of Fort Lauderdale. Like her sister, she created a clothing line, and she invests in other businesses as part of Serena Ventures. She has performed on TV, in movies, and, famously, in Beyoncé's video album *Lemonade*. She also devotes time and resources to giving back by helping children in need. Through her Serena Williams Fund, she has helped build a school in Kenya and a school in Jamaica, and has given scholarships to students in need.

Serena's commitment to her own health and concern for the well-being of others have pulled her into activism. In 2017, she married and became a mom. While giving birth to her daughter, Alexis Olympia, she faced a health crisis that could have taken her life. The experience showed her that women of color often don't receive the same quality of medical care given to other women. As a result, she has become a vocal advocate for black women around issues of health care. She is especially devoted to addressing the high rates of mortality among black mothers and their babies.

MEET VENUS!

Like her sister, Venus Williams is a force off and on the court. As a child, Venus had a 63–0 record on the United States Tennis Association junior tour and was ranked number one among the under-12 players in Southern California. In 2006, she published an essay in the London *Times* making the case for male and female champions being paid the same, something that up to then hadn't happened. Her efforts paid off for her and others. Venus became the first female tennis player to benefit from the equalization of prize money at Wimbledon when she won the tournament in 2007. In her career, she took the top spot at Wimbledon, one of the most prestigious tournaments in the sport, five times.

Eight months after giving birth, Serena was back in action at the French Open. In 2019, *Forbes* magazine ranked her as the highest paid woman athlete in the world. In everything she does, she demonstrates how preparation and conviction can combine to make a champion. In Serena's own words: "When I won my first championship, I was only 17 years old, but I never forgot that feeling. . . . There's really no feeling in the world like that." Serena also appreciates the importance of failure. "The only reason I am who I am is because of my losses, and some of them are extremely painful," she has said, "but I wouldn't take any of them away, because every time I lose, it takes a really long time for me to lose again because I learn so much from it." She encourages people to learn from their mistakes, not just in sports, but in business, school, or life. She says, "Don't live in the past, live in the present, and don't make the same mistakes in the future."

SISTERS, COMPETITORS, AND PARTNERS

Serena has played against Venus in 30 professional matches since 1998—and won 18 of those games. Together, they've won 14 Grand Slam doubles titles. They make a great team off the court too—in business. They became partial owners of the Miami Dolphins in 2009, making them the first African American women to have an ownership stake in a National Football League franchise. "In my life, it still and forever is always going to be Venus and Serena," says Serena. "She's my best friend, she's my soul mate. . . . On the court, we're mortal enemies. But the second we shake hands [after a match], we are best friends again."

"THE DAY I STOP FIGHTING FOR EQUALITY AND FOR PEOPLE THAT LOOK LIKE YOU AND ME WILL BE THE DAY I'M IN MY GRAVE."

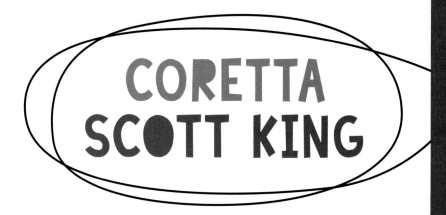

CORETTA SCOTT KING

Growing up, Coretta Scott imagined herself "seated next to the proverbial man in the moon, blasting off to adventures far past Heiberger," the Alabama town she called home. She picked cotton for $2 a week. Like other African Americans in the 1930s, she was forbidden from entering the front door of an ice cream parlor. She was forced to step off sidewalks to allow white people to pass, and she lived in constant fear of white violence. And what Coretta feared came to pass on Thanksgiving night in 1942. At 15 years old, she arrived home from choir rehearsal to find her house had been burned to the ground by white racists.

Like other black children, she asked her parents why they were hated by white people. Her mother told her, "You are just as good as anyone else. You get an education. Then you won't have to be kicked around." Coretta heeded her mother's advice. She worked hard, sang in church, and became the valedictorian of her high school class in 1945. After graduation, she enrolled in Antioch College, an integrated school where she studied education and voice. She also became active in the campus chapter of the NAACP.

When her time at Antioch ended, Coretta pursued music. She received a scholarship to attend the New England Conservatory, where she felt as if she "had blasted through that moonlit sky in Heiberger and touched the hem of heaven." She was living her dream, studying to be a concert singer. And, on the social side, she made friends, including one who introduced her to a young pastor named Martin Luther King Jr. When she first met him, she thought he was a bit young and short for her. But she recalled that on their first date, they "chatted about everything from questions of war and peace to racial and economic justice." They were married less than two years later. The wedding was held in Coretta's parents' yard in Marion, Alabama, in June 1953. Reverend King, the father of the groom, performed the ceremony.

For the rest of their lives, Coretta and Martin were bound together by love and their shared commitment to justice for all. As a young pastor, Martin was chosen to lead the Montgomery Bus Boycott in Coretta's home state in 1955 and 1956. Coretta helped start the Committee for a Sane Nuclear Policy in 1957—the same year Martin was elected president of the Southern Christian Leadership Conference (SCLC), one of the premier organizations of the civil rights movement. The couple worked together and separately and became two of the public faces of the movement.

Coretta dedicated herself to the causes she believed in, all while taking care of her husband and four children. She hosted family and community members in their home, and she traveled the world at her husband's side. The Kings were in Ghana to celebrate the country's independence from Britain in 1957. They went to India to study Mahatma Gandhi's methods of nonviolent protest in 1959. Coretta flew on her own to Switzerland as a delegate to the Women's Strike for Peace at an international disarmament conference in 1962, where she pleaded with US and Soviet leaders to sign a nuclear test ban treaty. And she was with Martin in Sweden when he received the Nobel Peace Prize in 1964.

Using her background in music and activism, Coretta also produced and starred in a series of Freedom Concerts, starting in 1964, to raise funds to support SCLC. She had her own ideas about how things were supposed to be. For example, she gave a speech at Madison Square Garden in June 1965 against the Vietnam War, saying, "Ultimately, there can be no peace without justice, and no justice without peace. The two great moral issues of our time, peace and human rights, are so closely related that we can say that they are one and the same."

Before Coretta and Martin were married, she had "the traditional language about 'obeying' and submitting to my husband" removed from her wedding vows.

Martin agreed with her anti-war stance. Up until then, he had focused on the push for equal rights under American law. But he began to speak on more international and economic issues. Martin was assassinated in 1968. Though devastated by the loss of her husband and best friend, Coretta remained active in the movement. Days after the tragedy, she led a march in her husband's place. A year later, as a tribute to Martin and his work, she founded an organization, the Martin Luther King, Jr. Center for Nonviolent Social Change in Atlanta. In 1974, she brought together 100 organizations, including civil rights and women's rights groups, business and labor associations, and religious organizations, to tackle the issue of unemployment. In the 1980s, she gathered together more than 800 human rights groups into the Coalition of Conscience for a demonstration commemorating the 20th anniversary of the March on Washington and her husband's iconic "I Have a Dream" speech.

> "We can end the violence of nuclear war, apartheid, racism, joblessness, terrorism, drugs, and the violence in our homes, in our schools, and in our streets if only we can find the will—and we must."

Her work did not end there. Coretta also championed the effort to make Dr. King's birthday a national holiday. She was active in South Africa's anti-apartheid movement for years, and she stood on the stage with Nelson Mandela as he was inaugurated as the country's first post-apartheid president in 1994. In the 1980s and 1990s, she began to support gay rights and marriage equality for same-sex couples. In a 1998 speech in Chicago, Coretta said, "Homophobia is like racism and anti-Semitism and other forms of bigotry in that it seeks to dehumanize a large group of people, to deny their humanity, their dignity, and personhood. This sets the stage for further repression and violence that spreads all too easily to victimize the next minority group."

Throughout her life, Coretta inspired countless people to join her in advocating for peace, equality, and economic justice. By the time she died in 2006, she had received honorary doctorates from more than 60 colleges and universities for her lifetime of service to humanity.

WHOOPI GOLDBERG

Before the world knew her as Whoopi Goldberg, she was Caryn Elaine Johnson. Caryn was a normal name for the "weird kid," as she described herself. Growing up in the 1960s, she didn't do things that people expected of her. "I wasn't into stockings. I couldn't dance. The subtle art of being a girl evaded me," she has said.

Whoopi grew up in the Chelsea-Elliot Houses, a housing project in New York City. From a young age, her mother, who worked as a nurse and a teacher, encouraged her daughter's interest in performing. She also understood that her daughter was bright and that she learned things differently than other kids did. Though she wasn't diagnosed until she was an adult, Whoopi had a learning disability, dyslexia, and did not do well in school. She left high school without graduating. In 1974, she moved across the country to California, where she worked with a theater company. She had another kind of education in mind. So she joined improvisation groups to hone her stand-up comedy skills.

HOW WHOOPI GOT HER STAGE NAME

Caryn Johnson's stage name came from the fact that she was, as she says, "a bit of a farter." She explained that the theaters she worked in were small and sometimes during a show she wouldn't have time to make it to the bathroom. "So if you get a little gassy," she has said, "you've got to let it go. So people used to say to me, 'You are like a whoopee cushion.'" She chose "Goldberg" from someone on her mother's side of the family.

It's hard to support yourself as an aspiring actress and comedian. So Whoopi worked odd jobs throughout her teens and twenties to make ends meet. She was a bricklayer, a garbage collector, and a bank teller. For a period, she even worked at a funeral home as a makeup artist for the dead as she continued to practice her craft.

Finally, in her thirties, she made her film debut in *Citizen: I'm Not Losing My Mind, I'm Giving It Away*. Soon after, she made her mark in a one-woman show she wrote called *The Spook Show*. In it, she portrayed characters rarely depicted on stage, including a disabled woman, a pregnant surfer, and a young black girl who imagines herself with blonde hair. She made the audience laugh but also made them think about the mistreatment of people who don't fit society's ideas of what is normal.

She developed the play in a house in Berkeley, California. Later, when she performed it in New York City at the Dance Theater Workshop, in the winter of 1983, she got a rave review that changed her life. Her talent caught the attention of a producer, who moved the show from a small theater downtown to a Broadway theater, where it was retitled *Whoopi Goldberg* to match her stage name. She had reached a whole new level.

While her show established her as a stand-up talent to watch, it was the film *The Color Purple* that made her a star. Whoopi played the lead role of Celie in the 1985 film, which also starred Oprah Winfrey (see page 118) and was based on the Pulitzer Prize–winning novel by Alice Walker (see page 66). The film was nominated for 11 Academy Awards, including one for Whoopi as Best Actress. Five years later, her next big box office hit, *Ghost*, earned her an Oscar for Best Supporting Actress. Whoopi did what few had done before her: she was a stand-up

WHOOPI IN SPACE!

Whoopi Goldberg made regular appearances on *Star Trek: The Next Generation*, starting in the late 1980s. She was a huge fan of the original *Star Trek*, which began in 1966, in part because it featured black actress Nichelle Nichols in the role of Lieutenant Uhura. Speaking with the show's creator, she asked, "Do you not know that, prior to your show, there were no black people in any sci-fi, anywhere?" She said that seeing a black woman on *Star Trek* made her think, "Oh, we are in the future." She said, "Uhura did that for me. So I want to be on your show."

> "I AM THE AMERICAN DREAM. . . . IT SAID YOU COULD COME FROM ANYWHERE AND BE ANYTHING YOU WANT IN THIS COUNTRY. THAT'S EXACTLY WHAT I'VE DONE."

comedian who found the kind of success in theater and film that made her one of the biggest stars in America.

But conquering stage and film was not quite enough for Whoopi. She is also the author of many books, starting with a retelling of *Alice in Wonderland*, in 1992, and followed by nearly a dozen more, including a six-book children's series called *Sugar Plum Ballerinas*. Her books for children and adults are like her work on stage—not only do they entertain, but they also inspire readers to think better of each other and themselves. They remind readers that people who are thought to be weird are really quite normal and worthy of kindness.

In her early fifties, when most megastars would have kicked up their feet and enjoyed the fruits of their labor, Whoopi took on something big and new to her. She joined daytime television as a talk show host leading the team at *The View*. Created by well-known journalist Barbara Walters, Whoopi and four other women talk, argue, share stories, interview guests, and entertain audiences with their range of opinions on politics, popular culture, and other hot topics of the day. In 2019, a writer for the *New York Times* called *The View* "the most important political TV show in America."

Whoopi is one of the few entertainers to earn an EGOT. That means she's won an Emmy, a Grammy, an Oscar, and a Tony Award.

HADIYAH-NICOLE GREEN

When Hadiyah-Nicole Green's aunt, Ora Lee Smith, was diagnosed with cancer, she said she would rather die than experience the side effects of the treatment her doctor offered. At first, Hadiyah didn't understand. Her aunt passed away. Three months later, her uncle, General Lee Smith, was diagnosed with cancer, and he chose to receive treatment. Taking care of her uncle, Hadiyah witnessed what she describes as "the horrors of cancer and the horrors of cancer treatment." When his doctors thought he would live for only a few more months, Hadiyah nursed him back to health and helped him live for 10 more years. "I watched him and took care of him as he went through chemotherapy and radiation," she said. "I watched him lose 150 pounds, all of his hair, his eyelashes, his eyebrows. I watched his fingernails turn black. And I saw how his skin went from being a beautiful chocolate to looking like it had been burnt in an oven or barbecued." She finally understood her aunt's decision.

When interviewed about the cancer treatment chemotherapy, Hadiyah said, "If you can imagine having one house on fire, chemo would be the equivalent of trying to put water over the whole city." The commonly used medicine acts against the diseased parts of the body, the tumors, but also destroys the healthy tissue nearby. She believed there had to be a better way to battle the disease.

Ora Lee and General Lee raised Hadiyah from the age of four in their St. Louis, Missouri, home. They made it possible for her to get the education she needed to earn a full scholarship to college. She graduated from Alabama A&M University in 2003 with an undergraduate degree in physics, with a concentration in optics and a minor in mathematics. After taking time off to care for her uncle, she earned her master of science degree in physics from the University of Alabama at Birmingham. Then she stayed at the university to complete her PhD in physics in 2012.

Hadiyah used her knowledge of science to explore a question: "If we can have a satellite in outer space communicate with just one cell phone in a room full of people, why can't we have that kind of precision when we're treating cancer in a person?" She thought laser technology might be a tool to do that. As a multidisciplinary physicist, Hadiyah specializes in using lasers, nanoparticles (microscopic objects), and antibodies (types of proteins in the body that fight things like bacteria or viruses that can harm a person) to target malignant tumors, create images of them, and treat them. Her approach, she explains, is "a targeted local therapy that treats just the tumor and not the rest of the body." Once again using a metaphor to explain, she says, "My treatment can come in and zoom in just on the one house on fire, without getting water on the rest of the neighbors."

In 2015, Hadiyah received a $1.1 million grant to support her research. She joined the faculty of the Morehouse School of Medicine in Atlanta, and she has founded a research organization that she named for her beloved aunt: the Ora Lee Smith Cancer Research Foundation (oralee.org). The organization's mission is to change the way cancer is treated for the better. "If I can be that one little voice to shine light on this literally with my laser and give accuracy and targeting with the precision of a laser pointer to treating cancer," she said, "we can just eliminate the tumor without having those side effects throughout the whole body."

The work has not been easy. She says many of her days were 20 hours long. "Most of the time, I worked seven days a week. And when I wasn't in the laboratory, I was either at church or at the gym," she shared. Sometimes she got discouraged. But a family member asked a question that kept her going: "What if you were the only person on the planet who could do this and you didn't do it?" Now Hadiyah is working to raise the funds she needs to move her treatment from the lab into human clinical trials. She hopes one day it can be used to provide low-cost, effective treatment to patients who need it.

"I've had too many breakthroughs the day or the week after I almost gave up. . . . It gives each of us a sense of responsibility to humanity to be obedient to our dreams."

AMY SHERALD

Amy Sherald was born to make art. In the second grade, she entertained herself in English class by drawing little pictures at the end of her sentences. She looked at paintings by the "Old Masters" (well-known European painters from the mid-thirteenth century to the mid-nineteenth century) in encyclopedias. Later, she took art classes in school and in private lessons after school. Despite her passion for the field, she didn't feel like art was something she was "supposed" to do professionally. Amy went to an art museum for the first time when she was in the sixth grade—but it didn't happen again until she was in college. Like many families where she grew up in Columbus, Georgia, her people were more into Bible study than going to museums and art events.

She took art classes at Spelman College while she earned her undergraduate degree at Clark Atlanta University. Then Amy got her master of fine arts degree (MFA) at Maryland Institute College of Art in Baltimore in 2004. But she decided to do something very different next. She trained to compete in a triathlon (a three-part race featuring biking, running, and swimming). She felt fit and healthy but decided to get a checkup before the race. That's when she found out she was suffering from cardiomyopathy, a form of heart disease.

A tough decade followed. She had been waiting tables to support herself but now the money would have to go toward medical expenses instead of her art career. And she had loved ones who were in need as well. Amy returned to Georgia to lend a hand to her mother and her aunts. But then her brother was diagnosed with cancer. Her hands were so full being a caretaker she didn't paint for several years.

When she was ready, she returned to her art practice and her day job in a restaurant in Baltimore. She carried on for a few years more before her heart condition caused her to fall ill. Doctors said she would need a heart transplant. She was receiving treatment in a hospital when she got the news of her brother's passing. A few days later, though, doctors confirmed that she would receive a new heart. "I didn't realize how strong I was until I lost my brother," Amy said. "And losing him only made me want to live my life even harder." Amy came through the transplant surgery with a renewed sense of purpose.

Like many other young artists, Amy pursued artist residencies and submitted her work for projects and exhibits. She found some success. Her work was hung at the Reginald F. Lewis Museum in Baltimore in 2013. But the competitive fine art market is more difficult than it appears. "In the beginning of your career," she explained, "your paintings could be selling for $8,000, $10,000, $12,000, but you're only making half of that." Gallery owners take a commission from every sale. Artists live on the rest. For an artist who finishes 10 or 11 paintings a year, "that's not that much money." On top of typical expenses like rent, food, and transportation, she had the costs of studio rental, paint, canvases, brushes, and other supplies.

Amy's big break came when she landed a solo exhibition in 2016 at the Monique Meloche Gallery in Chicago. Not only did her work sell, but she also had a waiting list of people who wanted to buy her paintings!

One of the things that makes Amy's style stand out is her use of shades of gray to create skin tone in her portraits of people. She does not use warm browns that people are more accustomed to seeing. She developed the approach the way many artists and scientists do: "by accident."

Amy's confidence in her style and her commitment to her craft paid off, even if it didn't please everyone. At first Amy's mother was confused

"DON'T COMPARE YOUR JOURNEY TO ANYBODY ELSE'S. FOCUS ON WHAT YOU NEED TO DO, BECAUSE YOUR PATH IS YOUR PATH."

INSPIRING ●THERS

Amy Sherald, the first black woman to paint an official portrait of a First Lady, is not only a critically acclaimed artist. She's also a role model. "For me, it's been important from the beginning that the works that I've made ended up in museums, so kids can see people who look like them in institutions," she has said. "Kids can look at my work and see somebody who looks like them and be empowered by that. I've gotten a lot of letters from kids who are interested in the arts or who weren't interested in art and are now engaging on a deeper level."

by her choice to pursue art. But by 2016, when Amy won a National Gallery Portrait Competition, her mother finally saw the wisdom in her daughter's choice. She said to Amy, "Oh my goodness, this is what you've been doing all these years! You're kind of a big deal!"

Neither of them knew that six months later, she'd be selected by First Lady Michelle Obama (see page 136) to paint her official portrait. The National Portrait Gallery commissioned Amy to create two copies of the portrait, which would hang in the White House and the National Portrait Gallery. As well as being a history-making first, "working with Michelle Obama was really fun," she shared. Since unveiling her striking portrait of the first African American First Lady, Amy's career has skyrocketed. "I am relieved that I can pay back my school loans," she said. But she's just as excited to discover that "kids know who I am now."

"PEOPLE WHO DON'T QUIT EVENTUALLY RISE TO THE TOP."

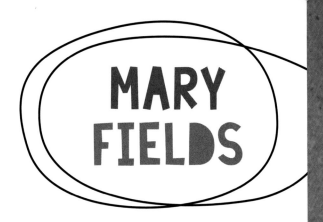

MARY FIELDS

Before email and the Internet, before plane routes and train lines connected cities to towns, people hand-delivered each other direct messages. They slipped handwritten letters into paper envelopes that were carried by people traveling on horses or in wagons. Mail carriers dodged thieves, galloped across cliffside roads, and faced tornadoes, snowstorms, raging waters, and muddy terrain to do their job. The historical image of these mail carriers is a lot like the fearless, gunslinging cowboys in Hollywood movies. But imagine this: at least one of those mail carriers in the late 1800s was a black woman named Mary Fields.

Born around 1832 in the South, she lived all of her childhood and young adult life enslaved. She was in her thirties in 1863 when the Emancipation Proclamation ended legal bondage in much of the South. Once liberated, she worked her way north on Mississippi riverboats. She found work as a groundskeeper at a Catholic convent in Toledo, Ohio. Both well-spoken and outspoken, she'd even argue with the nuns she worked for. By speaking up for herself, she managed to get better pay for the work she did. She was not well liked in the convent, except by Mother Amadeus, who was a leader in that religious community. In 1884, Mother Amadeus left the convent to go west to Montana Territory, where she felt there was greater work to be done. A year later, after Mary learned that Mother Amadeus was very sick, she went to her in Montana.

Mary was a woman who behaved in ways associated with men. She spoke her mind, drank whiskey, smoked cigars, wore men's style clothing, and didn't run away from a fight. Consequently, she was fired from her job at the convent in Montana. But Mary was not defeated. She was confident enough to accept a job delivering mail. She used a stagecoach given to her by Mother Amadeus to deliver mail between St. Peter's Mission and

Cascade, Montana. While working her route, she became known by many names, like Stagecoach Mary and White Crow—a name given to her by friends in the Blackfeet Nation.

All accounts describe her as a tall woman, wearing a skirt and apron or trousers and skilled at using the firearm that was always by her side. Mary moved about like a free woman. She was warm and generous, especially to children. She was memorable. Tami Charles, the author of a book called *Fearless Mary*, wrote, "The stagecoach is usually guarded by one person: the driver. To do the job, you need to be smart, tough, unshakable. As a former slave who traveled to the West alone to seek opportunity, Mary Fields is all of those things." She also described the dangers of Mary's job: "Outlaws prey on stagecoaches, which carry valuable supplies, money, and food. Wild animals prey on them too." Mary braved the weather and covered her route, often alone in her horse-drawn wagon, responsible for other people and their property. She had to protect herself from animals and humans who might mean harm.

There are no videos, of course, of Mary riding across the rugged landscapes. There are no recordings of her greeting the many people she must have met when bringing a long-awaited message to them. But we know she survived her journeys and lived to be around 82 years old. Toward the end of her life, historians say her temper cooled. She spent time in her garden and became a dedicated baseball fan. She gave flowers to neighbors and players who hit home runs and became a beloved member of the Cascade community. Though it can be difficult to separate the true events of her life from the lore about her, it's clear that Mary made an impression in her time. A few photographs of Mary still exist, and historians have documented her story of courage, freedom, and achievement. She left her mark in American history as a woman who did extraordinary things to transcend the horrors of the time and live as a self-determined black woman.

Many sources say that Mary once held back an entire pack of wolves with just her instincts and her rifle.

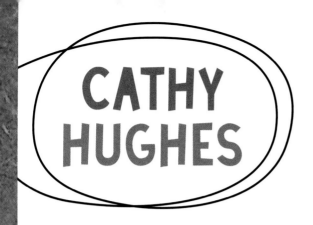

CATHY HUGHES

Growing up in Nebraska, Cathy Hughes's favorite thing to do was listen to the radio. As a young woman in the mid-1960s, she was also motivated by a desire to tell the stories of black people from their point of view. Fortunately for her, her hometown had a newspaper, the *Omaha Star*, and a radio station, KOWH. These black-owned media companies gave Cathy opportunities to gain work experience at an early age. She sold ads for 10 cents a word for the *Omaha Star* while still a teen and got a job at the radio station when she was just 21.

Cathy thought for a short time that her path to fulfilling her dream of having a career was derailed when she got pregnant at 16 and married her boyfriend. Rather than thwarting her ambitions, being a mother gave her a new motivation to continue pursuing her dream. The marriage lasted only a couple of years, but during that time, she completed high school and took some business courses.

While working at KOWH, she met Tony Brown, a dean in the communications department at Howard University in Washington, DC. He was so impressed with her drive that he offered her a job at the university. In 1973, she moved to the university's radio station, WHUR, and two years later, she was the station's vice president and general manager. While there, Cathy developed a new programming concept. The playlist she chose consisted of rhythm and blues (R&B) ballads— the kind of slow, romantic songs that appealed to black listeners at the time. The radio station moved from #35 to #3 in the ratings, an accomplishment that movers and shakers in the radio industry could not ignore. She called the new format "the Quiet Storm." It was wildly popular among listeners and eventually played on nearly 500 stations nationwide.

Cathy briefly worked at the country's first 24-hour gospel radio station, WYCB, in Washington, DC, before getting married again and launching Radio One, Inc. with her husband Dewey Hughes. In order to get their company started, they planned to buy the radio station WOL. But when they attempted to get a business loan, they were told "no" 32 times before they finally got a "yes." The marriage didn't last, but the 24-hour talk radio format they created was a winner. Cathy had long had the intention to provide black audiences, through radio, with knowledge and discussion that was meaningful to them— something the mainstream media neglected to do. After the marriage ended, she bought Dewey's shares in the radio station and took the lead.

> "We must exhibit the entrepreneurial spirit of our ancestors and not only be music innovators but also industry makers."

Cathy went through a lot to keep her dream alive. At one point, she and her young son moved into the radio station in order to keep expenses down. "I stayed focused on not losing my company . . . and did whatever it took," she said. "I was willing to let everything go except my son and my business, in that order." When she needed to economize, she became on-air talent and her station's biggest star. On her hit talk radio show, *The Cathy Hughes Show*, she interviewed leaders and innovators in the African American community.

Cathy's son, Alfred Liggins III, joined Radio One full-time in 1985, 19and 12 years later became the CEO of the company. Together, the mother-and-son team expanded the company, buying up other radio stations and creating the multimedia empire Urban One, Inc., which includes 56 radio stations and a cable television network called TVOne.

Cathy remains the face of the brand and a leader in her industry. She is a role model who has broken through glass ceilings and leapt over barrier after barrier. In 2018, she commented that she still saw an industry largely led by white men. She says that African Americans and women "cannot wait for the industry to change. We must be the change, as we have been so many times in the past." If the current leaders of an industry do not offer you a seat at the table, she says, you'll just have to create your own!

MAE JEMISON

"As a little girl growing up on the South Side of Chicago in the sixties," Mae Jemison said in a speech, **"I always knew I was going to be in space."** She was born in Decatur, Alabama, in 1956—the year before the Russians, ahead of everyone, successfully launched the first man-made satellite. Her family had moved to Chicago when she was three years old. Mae says she had "incredible teachers" in public school who encouraged students, including her, to pursue interests they otherwise may not have, such as in science and the arts. "I remember the sixties," she has said, "as this really creative time . . . when so many people were pushing to be a part of things." As examples, she pointed out that African nations were seeking independence from their European colonizers, women were launching a movement to achieve equality with men, and nations were competing to be the first and to travel the farthest in space.

Mae came of age watching television shows like *Star Trek*, which were inspired by space travel. She loved reading, especially about archaeology and astronomy. And she loved keeping up with news coverage of NASA and the space program. At night, she could often be found staring up into the starry night sky.

Mae was also interested in dance. When she went to Stanford University in California, in 1973, she honed her skills as a dancer and choreographer, while studying chemical engineering and African and Afro-American studies. She graduated four years later and then moved east to go to Cornell University Medical College in New York City (now known as Weill Cornell Medicine). Though she loved to dance, she decided that science would be her professional path. In a radio interview, she shared, "My mother said you can always dance if you're a doctor but you can't necessarily doctor if you're a dancer." She studied medicine in New

SCIENCE LITERACY

Mae Jemison is devoted to promoting science literacy for everyone. She doesn't mean that "you have to be a professional scientist or technologist to be science literate." But rather, she has said she wants people to be "able to understand the world going on around you, to be able to read an article in the newspaper about the environment, about toxins, about health to be able to figure out how to vote on it." Even if you are not involved in the sciences, she argues, you may be able to weigh in on what problems need solving and what projects should get funding or attention.

York and took her medical skills on the road, volunteering in Cuba and Kenya and at a refugee center in Thailand. After graduation, Mae practiced medicine in Los Angeles before spending a few years in Sierra Leone and Liberia in West Africa, working with the Peace Corps.

Mae had a successful career in medicine, but she also had a dream that remained unfulfilled: space travel. She applied to NASA's astronaut training program and was one of 15 aspiring astronauts chosen from a pool of about 2,000 applicants.

In September 1992, Mae was a crew member of the space shuttle *Endeavour*. The first African American woman astronaut in space, she spent eight days working in Spacelab, NASA's Earth-orbiting science laboratory, carrying out a joint mission between the United States and Japan. As the science mission specialist, she ran experiments concerned with the reproduction of frogs and the development of tadpoles in space. She also studied space adaptation syndrome, the type of motion sickness that astronauts experience in the absence of gravity.

Mae's achievement was groundbreaking not only for herself, but for all black people. She acknowledged the significance of her place in history by taking objects representing African and African American culture with her into space. She brought along a photograph of black pioneer pilot Bessie Coleman (see page 126) and a poster of dancer Judith Jamison performing *Cry*, a signature piece choreographed by Alvin Ailey. She also carried into space a Bundu statue from a West African secret society for women and a flag representing Alpha Kappa Alpha, her sorority. She wanted to recognize African Americans who had so often been overlooked by scientific institutions, hoping that her step forward would pave the way for others. Always looking to the future, Mae is now part of a project called 100 Year Starship, an initiative whose mission is "to make the capability of human travel beyond our solar system a reality within the next 100 years."

By the age of three, Eunice Kathleen Waymon was playing her family's piano. "I remember playing a song, 'God Be with You Till We Meet Again' in the key of F," she said in an interview. "Of course, I didn't know what the key was," she continued, "I didn't get interested in music. It was a gift from God." Her parents and everyone in the community of Tryon, North Carolina, agreed that she was extraordinarily gifted. They encouraged her and contributed money for her lessons.

Eunice played in piano recitals where people outside of her community could hear her talent. And she began to see the realities of the wider world. Once, she looked up from the piano as she performed in a recital to see her parents being removed from their seats in the front row to make room for a white family. As she recalled in her memoir, she stood up in her "starched dress" and made it clear that "if anyone expected to hear me play, then they'd better make sure that my family was sitting right there in the front row where I could see them." Her parents were returned to the front.

After Eunice finished school in North Carolina, she went to New York City to study for a year at Juilliard, one of the great music schools in the Northeast. She moved on and auditioned for a scholarship spot at the Curtis Institute of Music in Philadelphia. Going to school in Philly would allow her to save money by living with relatives. Sadly, she was rejected. To her, it felt like "the end of everything." She didn't have the money to find another school, but she had not lost her talent or her passion. She still dreamed of becoming a concert pianist.

Eunice needed to make money. She found a job as a photographer's assistant. Then she worked at a vocal studio. She gave some private vocal lessons. The better paying jobs for musicians, though, were found in nightclubs, playing jazz and standards, something she had no problem doing—she could play anything. But if her parents found out that she worked in places where people smoked and drank and partied at all hours of the night, they would be unhappy. Her mother thought of jazz as "the devil's music." Eunice did not want to disappoint her but couldn't pass up the opportunities that were coming her way. So she decided to take a stage name. That's how Eunice Waymon became Nina Simone. Her new first name came from the Spanish word *niña*, meaning "little girl." It was a nickname given to her by a boyfriend. Her new last name came from a French actress who inspired her: Simone Signoret. The name stuck as she became a big star.

After moving to Atlantic City, New Jersey, in 1954, she began working for a club owner who insisted that she play the piano *and* sing— something she'd only done in church. Her voice was just as powerful outside of church as it was inside! The crowds and club owners loved her. Word spread fast that she was a musician to check out, no matter the genre. She could play in a wide range of styles—including folk, soul, blues, jazz, and classical—and she made fans of people from all kinds of backgrounds and tastes. She sang with feeling that came from someplace deep inside her.

She recorded a demo of the songs she performed and sent it around to music executives. One day, in 1957, a music industry representative heard Nina sing live in Atlantic City. He brought her to a studio in New

LIVE FROM CARNEGIE HALL

Nina Simone's lifelong aspiration was to be a concert pianist. When she played the prestigious venue Carnegie Hall, she wrote a letter to her parents. She told them she was finally performing where they wanted her to perform, but she said she should've been playing Bach, her favorite composer. "I loved the audience," she said. "But, I wasn't playing classical music. And I wanted to be."

York City, where they recorded songs, including "I Loves You, Porgy," from the opera *Porgy and Bess.* The song tells the story of a woman torn between two men, one who is kind and one who's mean. Nina sang the song in a lower key than most singers before her. She slowed down the tempo and created her first hit.

Nina rose to prominence in the 1960s and 1970s, at the height of the civil rights and Black Power movements, which influenced her as an African American and an artist. Nina infused her music with the messages of the movement. In "Four Women," she sings about women who are different shades of blackness, and audiences felt that she was speaking for every black woman.

Nina produced sounds that were smooth as honey, guttural and piercing, or bright and hopeful. Her song "To Be Young, Gifted, and Black," written in memory of her friend Lorraine Hansberry (see page 29), was an anthem for African Americans. Nina wrote the music. Her bandleader, Weldon Irvine, wrote the lyrics, including: "My joy of today, is that we can all be proud to say, to be young, gifted, and black, is where it's at." Her intention with the song was to "make black children all over the world feel good about themselves, forever."

"We are the most beautiful creatures in the whole world: black people. I mean that in every sense, outside and inside. To me, we have a culture that is surpassed by no other civilization. But, we don't know anything about it. . . . My job is to somehow make them curious enough or persuade them, by hook or crook, to get more aware of themselves and where they came from . . . and what is already there."

Nina's memoir, *I Put a Spell on You*, shares a title with one of her most memorable songs. The song was written by Screamin' Jay Hawkins.

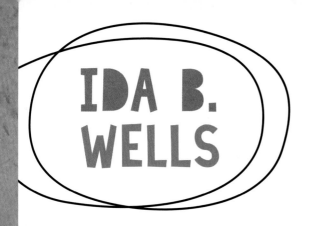

IDA B. WELLS

Ida B. Wells was a baby in 1863 when President Abraham Lincoln issued the Emancipation Proclamation, which freed all enslaved people in the rebellious Southern states. Ida's parents, James and Lizzie Wells, fared better than many African Americans in the transition from enslavement to freedom. Ida wrote in her memoir, *Crusade for Justice*, "My father had been taught the carpenter's trade, and my mother was a famous cook. . . . They had no trouble in finding plenty of [paying] work to do." Many African Americans were not so lucky. They were liberated without the resources to acquire land, money, or an education.

Neither Ida's mother nor her father was literate because it had been illegal for enslaved people to learn to read and write. So when Ida and her siblings went to school, their mother studied right alongside them. The family thrived, living in Holly Springs, Mississippi, in a nice home with all they needed—until an outbreak of yellow fever hit. It took the lives of James and Lizzie, and also killed Ida's nine-month-old baby brother.

Friends and neighbors gathered to discuss who would care for the orphaned Ida and her young brothers and sisters. But no one family was able to keep all six siblings together. Ida believed that separating the children would cause their parents to "turn over in their graves." So, at age 14, she took on the role of parent, keeping her siblings together in the home their parents had provided for them. She commuted six miles by mule to the one-room schoolhouse where she worked as a teacher, coming home on the weekends to care for her family.

In 1881, after two years at the country school, Ida moved to Memphis with two of her sisters to live with an aunt. Her new job was far enough away that she

> **"The way to right wrongs is to turn the light of truth upon them."**

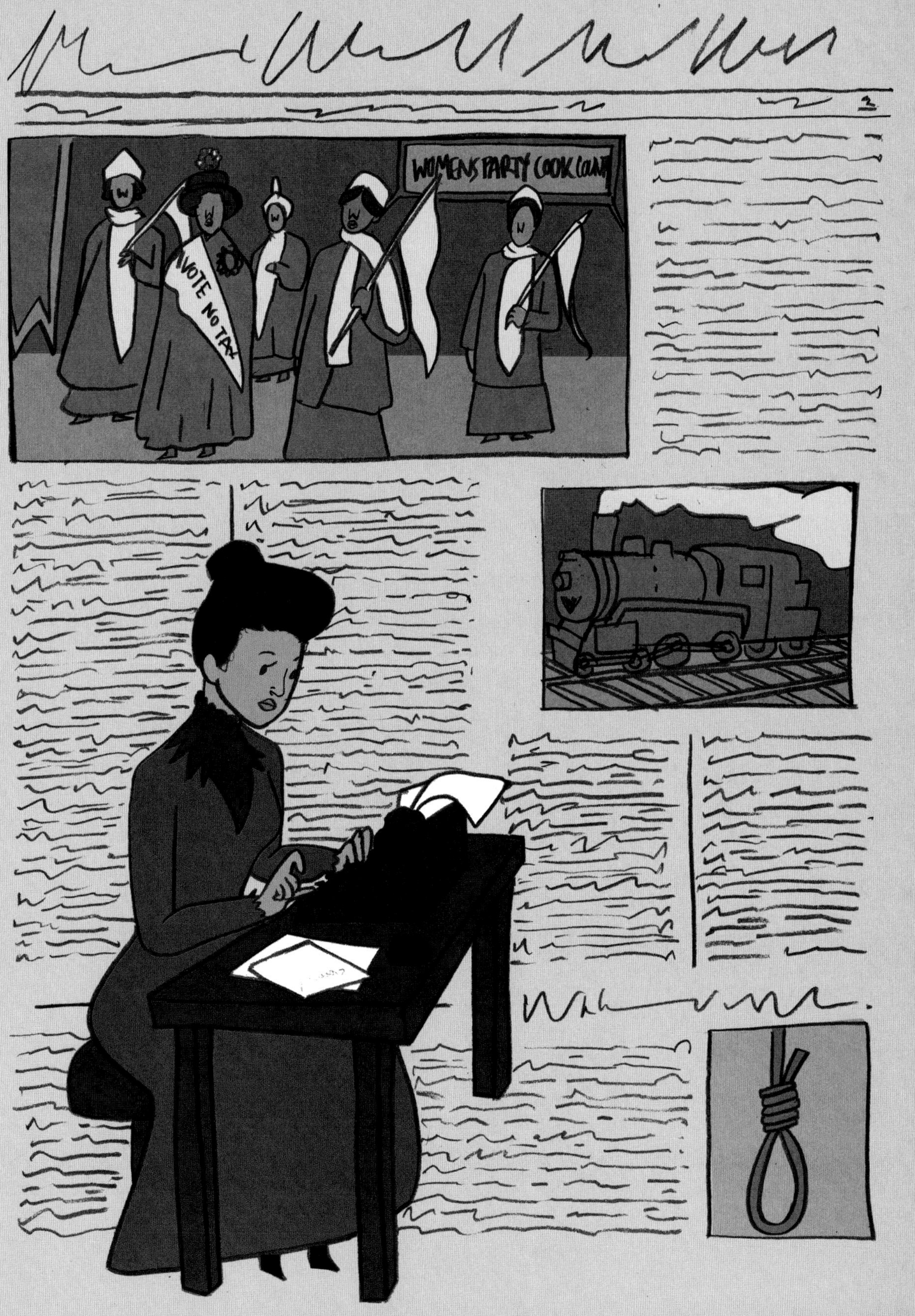
WOMENS PARTY COOK COUNTY
VOTE NO TAX

had to commute by train. In the years after slavery ended in the South, many local laws, known as Jim Crow laws, made the rules different for black and white people. Although these laws violated the Fourteenth Amendment, which guaranteed equal protection, they were still in place. So at any given time, a white person on a whim or in a bad mood had the privilege of denying a black person's rights.

Ida didn't take this hardship lying down. In September 1883, she bought a first-class ticket and took her seat in the ladies' coach, where she usually sat among black and white women. When the train's conductor came around to collect tickets, he refused to take hers and insisted she go sit in the second-class car. When she remained in her seat, he grabbed her arm to drag her from the train car. After she bit him, he called for two other men, who forced her out of the seat. Rather than ride in a second-class car, Ida got off the train at the next station, determined to take legal action.

Ida's battle against Jim Crow laws did not end there. Knowing that she had the same rights as any other American citizen according to the law, she sued the railroad and won a settlement of $500. The railroad company appealed—meaning they took the lawsuit to a higher court—and the decision was reversed. This time, the court decided in favor of the railroad, and Ida did not receive the $500. The justice system failed, but Ida was emboldened to challenge the system and devote herself to activism.

An avid reader and writer, she accepted an invitation in 1889 to write for the *Free Speech and Headlight*, a black newspaper in Memphis. She loved the work so much that she bought one-third of the newspaper and became its editor, shortening its name to the *Free Speech*. Then, after years of working as both a teacher and a journalist, Ida was fired from her teaching job for writing about the sorry state of black-only schools. Ida was now free to travel to research stories outside of Memphis and to promote the paper, expanding its readership to the states around Tennessee.

She was in Natchez, Mississippi, in 1892, when she got word from Memphis that three black men she knew had been lynched. She returned to Memphis, and her paper's coverage of the lynching outraged local white residents, who formed a mob and destroyed the *Free Speech*'s offices. They also threatened Ida's life. She was heartbroken. "It came just as I had demonstrated that I could make a living by my newspaper and need never tie myself down to school teaching," she wrote. The racist act of terrorism created a professional and personal setback for Ida. But only for a short time.

Ida left the South for her safety. But she also "saw the chance to be of more service to the cause by staying in New York." She took a position at another newspaper, the *New York Age*. Her dedication to reporting on lynching and other acts of racial terror gave rise to a mass movement against lynching. In her 1909 speech "Lynching, Our National Crime," she called lynching a "blight upon our nation, mocking our laws, and disgracing our Christianity" and laid out many ways the government could use its power to prevent atrocities like these from ever happening again. Ida took her anti-lynching activism as far as the United Kingdom, where her pamphlet "Southern Horrors" was sold to raise funds and gain the support of the British.

Ida was nothing short of extraordinary. Born into the last generation of enslaved African Americans, she managed to have a rewarding career, a great marriage, and four children. She traveled the country alone and went overseas when women had little protection under the law— and black people had none. She set an example that inspired African Americans and women to excel in journalism and business. A leader of a mass movement for justice that saved lives, she commanded respect and achieved international recognition at a time when masses of black people were rendered silent and powerless in their own country.

"I FELT THAT ONE HAD BETTER DIE FIGHTING AGAINST INJUSTICE THAN TO DIE LIKE A DOG OR A RAT IN A TRAP."

ZORA NEALE HURSTON

When Zora Neale Hurston's father learned about a town founded and governed by African Americans, he moved his family from Alabama to Florida to make it their home. Zora was a toddler at the time. The town, named Eatonville, offered African American families a safe place to raise their children, practice their trades, run their own businesses, and gather peacefully for fellowship and fun without fear of discrimination or abuse. Safe havens like Eatonville were incredibly rare in the era of Jim Crow laws (oppressive laws that restricted the freedoms of black Americans after the end of slavery). Zora and her siblings lived in a home built by their father on land he bought. Their house was surrounded by citrus and guava trees and a vegetable garden. "We were never hungry," she wrote in her autobiography, *Dust Tracks on a Road*. "We had chicken on the table often; home-cured meat, and all the eggs we wanted."

Zora's childhood was wonderful in many ways, but it was not without difficulties. When she will still a girl, her mother fell sick and died. Less than a year after her mother's death, her father remarried—too soon for Zora's liking. She never bonded with her stepmother, and her older siblings, already grown, were out of the house. Feeling unwelcome at home, she was sent to live with family friends. She then lived with one of her brothers, then the next, until she chose to set out on her own. Zora supported herself by cleaning people's homes. She was then hired as a maid to a woman who performed with a theater troupe. When the group headed north along the East Coast, Zora went too.

A curious child, Zora enjoyed reading and studying when she lived at home. But after leaving Eatonville, she did not have steady access to books or schools. When the troupe stopped in Baltimore, where one of her sisters lived, she decided to stay and go back to school. She went to Morgan Academy, the high school division of what's currently known as Morgan State University. After Morgan, she went to Howard University in nearby Washington, DC. To pay her tuition, she worked as a waitress in a nightclub and a manicurist in a barbershop—great places to observe people and collect stories.

Zora had grown up listening to people tell their stories—or *lies*, as she called them—on the porch of Eatonville's general store. More and more, she wanted to write the stories. She and some fellow writers at Howard founded a campus newspaper, *The Hilltop*. Her writing appeared there and in a campus literary magazine called *The Stylus*. She loved the university but couldn't bear the financial burden long enough to finish. So she headed to New York City to take a chance on living the life of a writer. She was far from alone in her aspirations for big things in the big city. The Great Migration of black people out of the former slave states of the South was underway, and the country would never be the same. There was a new surge of creativity in the black community. So much exciting, new work was being produced, particularly by African American artists and thinkers, that the explosion of culture in the 1920s came to be identified as the Harlem Renaissance.

Zora soon found her place as an emerging literary talent. *Opportunity*, an influential literary magazine, published a short story by her and later presented her with an award in two categories: fiction and drama. At the award presentation, she made such an impression that one of the

"FOLKLORE IS THE ARTS OF THE PEOPLE BEFORE THEY FIND OUT THAT THERE IS ANY SUCH THING AS ART."

judges, novelist Fannie Hurst, offered her a job as a secretary. And one of the guests, Annie Nathan Meyer, an author and women's education advocate, got her a full scholarship to Barnard College. There Zora studied anthropology, the branch of the social sciences that focuses on the language, culture, and behavior of humans. The discipline fit with her desire to explore and document black folklore, her own culture. Studying anthropology required her to do fieldwork, to get out of the library and study her subjects in the real world. She called it "poking and prying with a purpose." She did what women rarely did at the time—she drove a car and traveled alone. She went throughout the South and visited the islands of the Caribbean. She spent time with miners, lumberjacks, farmers, guitar players, hoodoo doctors, and more. She wrote her most famous novel, *Their Eyes Were Watching God*, while doing fieldwork in Haiti. It was set in her hometown of Eatonville, a place that was home to a people who were never far from her heart.

ZORA REDISCOVERED

Zora Neale Hurston was nearly forgotten for decades after her death, except by anthropologists and academics. One such teacher who mentioned Zora in class was Margaret Walker Alexander, a celebrated poet and author of *Jubilee*, an epic novel. Among Margaret's students was writer Alice Walker (see page 66), who was so moved by Zora's work and life that she went to Florida to find Zora's resting place. Finding her grave unmarked, Alice had a marker made. It reads:

Zora Neale Hurston
"A Genius of the South"
1901–1960
Novelist, Folklorist, Anthropologist

Alice helped introduce Zora's work to a new generation of readers and publishers. Now all of Zora's titles are in print and widely read. In fact, in 2018, a never-before published work of Zora's found new life. Completed in 1931, *Barracoon* is the story of one of the last Africans to be brought on a slave ship to America.

SISTER ROSETTA THARPE

Rosetta Atkins's gift for music was revealed early. She got her training in the Church of God in Christ (COGIC) in Cotton Plant, Arkansas, where her mother, Katie, was a singer, musician, and traveling missionary. Born in 1915, Rosetta was making music when she was three years old. "I remember that my mother set me on her knees when she played the harmonium at church," she once told an interviewer. "I would tap 'Nearer My God to Thee' with a single finger, and my mother accompanied me with her left hand." She was six years old when her mother left her father and moved the two of them to Chicago. That same year, the mother-daughter pair began performing onstage together at the COGIC churches around town and farther afield. Young Rosetta sang songs like "The Day Is Past and Gone" with the maturity of a grown-up. Word about her remarkable gift spread from one black community to another. Soon the youngster had fans by the thousands in churches around the country.

Sacred music was a family affair for the Atkinses. And Rosetta stood out, with the way she sang and her strong guitar-playing skills. On top of that, she was known for catching the holy spirit. She shouted and danced in the traditional way African Americans praise God. She was an exciting girl to watch.

In 1934, when she was 19 years old, Rosetta married Thomas Tharpe, a preacher who was a part of her church community. Her husband preached, but she was the one who drew the crowds. She left the marriage after a few years, and in 1938, she accepted a record deal with Decca Records. The label was excited to have a gospel musician singing in such a new and popular style. (Members of her church were not so happy about her singing their songs for a secular, or non-religious, audience.) Decca released four songs by "Sister"

Rosetta Tharpe—"The Lonesome Road," "Rock Me," "That's All," and "My Man and I"—and they all became instant hits. Though she never abandoned the church or sacred music, she did launch a new phase of her career, performing secular music onstage and in nightclubs. Some members of her church community were hurt by this. They criticized Rosetta for wearing flamboyant clothes, performing in places they found inappropriate, and mocking their church traditions. Despite the controversy, Rosetta's mother stuck by her daughter.

In 1941, Rosetta signed a contract with bandleader Lucky Millinder, who was known for spotting talent. With his orchestra, she recorded songs including "Shout, Sister, Shout!" and "Tall Skinny Papa." These songs were hugely popular but got her in even more trouble with her religious community. After two years, Rosetta left the big band behind. She went back to singing gospel in a more traditional way, still with her own style. She kept her old fans, gained new ones, and brought her unique brand of gospel music to the masses. "Strange Things Happening Every Day," released in 1945, months before the end of World War II, was the biggest hit of her career.

"All this new stuff they call rock 'n' roll—why, I've been playing that for years now."

The following spring, she met a performer named Marie Knight and was so impressed with her singing that she partnered with her to make another big hit called "Up Above My Head." Rosetta and Marie were wonderful as artists on their own and even better together. They spent years working together, often traveling and performing as a popular duet—another chapter in the remarkable story of Rosetta's life.

Throughout her unconventional career, Rosetta played with blues and jazz greats, like master composer Duke Ellington. She performed religious songs all over the South with bands like the Dixie Hummingbirds, a popular gospel group that brought great energy wherever they went. She broke the rules of racial segregation and performed with white musicians, such as the famous quartet the

Sister Rosetta Tharpe was inducted to the Rock and Roll Hall of Fame in 2018.

Jordanaires. No matter what Rosetta brought to the stage, it was fire. Fans lined up around corners, and audiences packed venues. She had legions of devoted fans among soldiers in World War II.

In addition to being an exceptional musician, Rosetta also understood the value of showmanship. In the late 1940s, for example, when her popularity was waning, she looked for a way to boost her profile. Approached by concert promoters, she agreed to stage her wedding in a stadium during a show in 1951. More than 20,000 fans witnessed her marriage to Russell Morrison, a man who worked in the music business. Guests paid admission, from $0.90 to $2.50. Rumor had it that Morrison was living off her fame and fortune, but they remained together for 22 years.

Rosetta took black gospel music out of the church and into the mainstream and influenced generations of artists who came after her, notably Elvis Presley. Her guitar work on "Down by the Riverside" can be heard in the music that made Jimi Hendrix a legend. The greats of the twentieth century, including Chuck Berry, Nina Simone (see page 98), Van Morrison, and Eric Clapton, count her as an inspiration. Bob Dylan called her a "force of nature." Her career continued until nearly the end of her life. She made her last recording in 1968 and passed away in 1973, known as the Godmother of Rock and Roll.

A TRUE TRAILBLAZER

About Sister Rosetta Tharpe, blues and rock musician Bonnie Raitt said, "[She] blazed a trail for the rest of us women guitarists with her indomitable spirit and accomplished, engaging style. She has long been deserving of wider recognition and a place of honor in the field of music history."

TOURING IN THE SOUTH

Sister Rosetta Tharpe traveled across the South performing her music. At the time, everything was segregated: water fountains, public restrooms, movie theaters, and more. Rosetta was a star, but like any other black person in the segregated South, she could not stay in a hotel or eat in a restaurant's dining room. She was often accompanied by another female singer, someone she could become friends with and share the good times and bad times with on the road. When they were hungry, the singers might find a restaurant where they could buy a meal. They could enter through the back door, but they had to take their food back to their bus because they weren't allowed to sit inside with the white patrons.

SHIRLEY FRANKLIN

As an 18-year-old college freshman, Shirley Clarke went to the 1963 March on Washington in the nation's capital with her mother, aunts, and cousins. This pivotal event in the civil rights movement became one of the most memorable experiences of her youth. Shirley's family walked with hundreds of thousands of people who shared the same concerns for the well-being of all Americans—particularly African Americans, who were still fighting for legal equality and justice. Shirley was moved by the profound messages of the march, especially by the words of Martin Luther King Jr., who delivered his famous "I Have a Dream" speech that day. King said, "I have a dream that one day down in Alabama—with its vicious racists, with its governor having his lips dripping with the words of interposition and nullification—one day right there in Alabama, little black boys and black girls will be able to join hands with little white boys and white girls as sisters and brothers." Like so many others who heard those words, Shirley was touched and motivated.

Born in 1945 in Philadelphia, she received an undergraduate degree in sociology from Howard University and a master's degree in sociology from the University of Pennsylvania. Then Shirley was pulled south by a teaching job. She spent nearly 10 years as a political science professor at Talladega College in Alabama before moving to Atlanta. She married a man from there who shared her interest in politics and social justice, David McCoy Franklin, who joined a firm with another dynamic young lawyer named Maynard Jackson. Shirley and David raised three children while encouraging local African Americans to go into business and to

> "My mother was a teacher and she instilled in me that one of the most important assets in life was an education."

become active in politics. In fact, David helped Maynard get elected as Atlanta's first black mayor in 1973.

A few years later, Mayor Jackson appointed Shirley as the director of the city's Bureau of Cultural Affairs. Shirley made a great contribution to the city, and her role in the administration grew. She became the commissioner of the Department of Cultural Affairs, a cabinet position in the administration. Mayor Jackson got credit for expanding opportunities for women and black people across the city. His administration pushed for laws requiring government officials to hire minority professionals. It also commissioned the work of minority artists and gave them grants. After serving for eight years, he could not run again in 1981 (term limits allow only two back-to-back terms), so Shirley stayed on to work as the chief administrative officer for the next mayor, Andrew Young. Mayor Jackson ran again in 1989, and Shirley was by his side during his third term, this time as the executive officer for operations. She credits these two prior mayors for inspiring her, saying, "They taught me how to be a leader, to follow my conscience, to act with foresight and courage." And, she says, they convinced her to run for office.

In 2002, Shirley became the 58th mayor of Atlanta—the city where Martin Luther King Jr. was born and made his home. She was the first black female mayor of a major southern city. Three years after she took office, *Time* magazine named Shirley one of the "five best big-city mayors." It credited her with restoring the city's faith in its government after the troubled tenure of Mayor Bill Campbell, who preceded her. She worked with the city council to establish a new code of ethics for city employees. She convinced 75 non-government firms to conduct studies of how the city spent its money; how it developed roads, facilities, and systems; and how it could solve the problem of homelessness. And she

> **"As an African American female mayor of a major US city, I am evidence that while progress may not always be swift, it is possible."**

Before Shirley Franklin, there was Sharon Pratt Kelly. She was the first black woman to lead a big American city. She served as mayor of Washington, DC, from 1991 to 1995.

convinced many of them to offer their expert suggestions at no cost to the city. She demonstrated how resources outside of government could be used by government.

During her two terms in office, Shirley enacted much-needed reforms and tackled a serious budget shortfall head-on. She streamlined the court system to save money and improved the general operations of the courts. And she led the efforts to overhaul the city's sewer system, so sewage would no longer flow into the city's rivers during heavy rains (yuck!). Shirley's accomplishments earned her recognition by the John F. Kennedy Library Foundation, which gave her their 2005 Profile in Courage Award. This was a first for a mayor in office, male or female. In her acceptance speech, she explained, "The city faced a 20 percent budget gap, a dilapidated and underfunded water and sewer system, and hundreds of dispirited employees. But with hard work and persistence, we balanced the budget and funded the $3 billion water infrastructure."

Shirley is a tremendous role model, inspiration, and advisor to a new generation of women, particularly in business and politics. She speaks and teaches on campuses and advises executives. And to this day, she draws on the inspiration of Martin Luther King Jr., saying his "life and his death are a lesson in respecting the dignity of every living being." She is the executive chairman of the board of directors of Purpose Built Communities, a nonprofit organization involved in providing early childhood education and mixed-income housing so that people who have less will not be stuck in struggling neighborhoods. She was also co-chair of the Democratic National Convention's 2016 platform committee, working on what she described as "a bold vision for working families, social justice, and the continuing prosperity and security of our country."

"EVERY GENERATION MAKES A MARK ON HISTORY."

OPRAH WINFREY

Oprah Winfrey wasn't always first-name famous and living her best life. Her childhood was marked by ups and downs and moving from one household to another. Her mother, Vernita Lee, left her in the care of her grandmother on a rural farm in Mississippi, while she got herself established in Milwaukee, Wisconsin. Oprah's grandmother, Hattie Mae Lee, showed her love and taught her to read. But life in such a remote place was lonely for a little girl. Plus, Hattie Mae was strict and quick to give out punishment for any disobedience. Her expectations of Oprah were high. So it was not surprising when Oprah, who had been reading since she was three, skipped kindergarten. Her teachers placed her in first grade when she was five years old.

When Oprah was six years old, Vernita brought her daughter to live with her in Milwaukee, where she had found steady work. The pay was low, though, and that made living in a neighborhood plagued by poverty and crime their only option. The joy and freedom Oprah felt as she ran and played on the farm was over. After an unhappy year in Milwaukee, Oprah was moved again, this time to live with her father, Vernon Winfrey, a barber in Nashville, Tennessee. She spent a year with him before returning to her mother for several more difficult years. At the age of 14, she returned to Nashville. As an independent businessman, Vernon was better able to provide for her. Like her grandmother, he was loving and strict. He had lots of rules, such as requiring Oprah to write book reports every week and insisting she learn new vocabulary words every day. But the household was stable, and she was safe.

> **Oprah received the nation's highest civilian honor, the Presidential Medal of Freedom, from President Barack Obama in 2013.**

In Tennessee, she was active in the drama club and debate club. She performed with and for other students (back on her grandmother's farm, animals were often Oprah's only audience). Always outgoing, Oprah became a leader. She served on the student council and, in 1970, entered a speaking competition sponsored by the Elks Club and won. Her prize? A four-year college scholarship that assured her an education and left her feeling like she could follow her dreams. She began working at a radio station as a high school student. With a talent for radio, and being a natural on TV, she became the youngest news anchor—and first black woman anchor—at a local Nashville TV station while she was a student at Tennessee State University.

In 1976, Oprah moved to Baltimore, Maryland, where she co-anchored the news before becoming the co-host of a show called *People Are Talking*. That job led to another as a host on a morning show, *AM Chicago*. She quickly discovered how much she fed off other people's energy and preferred a show with a live audience. She said, "I needed people. I needed to have you to gauge how things were going during the show, if you were responding, if you were laughing, if you were tracking with me." After that first show, the crew starting setting up folding chairs. "We brought in the staff, secretaries, anybody we could find in the building, and filled the first rows with staff people and the rest with people off the street that we bribed with doughnuts and coffee." Viewers loved her.

In 1985, two things happened that changed Oprah's life. First, she was asked to expand her show to be an hour long and change the name to *The Oprah Winfrey Show*. Second, she appeared in the movie version of *The Color Purple*, the best-selling novel by Alice Walker (see page 66). Her powerful performance earned her an Oscar win and a Golden Globe nomination and introduced her to a huge audience of new fans. When *The Oprah Winfrey Show* debuted as a nationally syndicated show (a show that can be shown on many different TV networks) in September 1986, it was a hit! And it stayed at the top of the national charts for 25 seasons. That same year, she formed a company called Harpo Productions ("Harpo" is "Oprah" spelled backward) and made sure she had a big financial stake in the show and lots of creative control. Looking back, Oprah said she

There are 4,561 episodes of *The Oprah Winfrey Show*.

remembered a colleague telling her "one station manager said that he'd rather put a potato in a chair in his market than have a big black girl with a funny name. And in spite of that, from Memphis to Macon, from Pittsburgh to Pensacola, from New York to New Orleans, you all let me in."

In 2000, she launched *O: The Oprah Magazine*. Oprah's career as an on-air television personality and actress paired well with her savvy business sense and helped her build a media empire. Ready for a change, Oprah ended *The Oprah Winfrey Show* in 2011 to focus on her biggest and most ambitious venture, the Oprah Winfrey Network (OWN). OWN broadcast unscripted shows, such as *Dr. Phil* and Iyanla Vanzant's *Iyanla: Fix My Life*, that offered audiences inspirational, self-help, and self-improvement advice. Oprah later added hit scripted dramas, like *Queen Sugar* and *Greenleaf*, which have both received critical praise. Already accomplished beyond her childhood dreams, she also continued to act in movies, including *The Butler*, *Selma*, and *A Wrinkle in Time*.

Oprah has not only achieved a lot, but she also has remained committed to giving to others. Because she endured abuse as a child, she testified in Washington, DC, in support of the National Child Protection Act, a bill that required a nationwide database of convicted child abusers. The act was signed into law by President Bill Clinton in 1993 and nicknamed the "Oprah Bill." A talk with human rights leader Nelson Mandela when she visited South Africa in the early 2000s led her to create the Oprah Winfrey Leadership Academy for Girls. The school, which opened in 2007, serves children in grades 8 to 12, ensuring a better chance for young black girls to reach and surpass their goals.

"KEEP A GRATITUDE JOURNAL. EVERY NIGHT, LIST FIVE THINGS THAT HAPPENED THIS DAY, IN DAYS TO COME, THAT YOU ARE GRATEFUL FOR."

SHIRLEY CHISHOLM

In the 1920s, the Caribbean suffered from widespread crop failure and food shortages. That led to mass migrations of people from the islands to the United States. Shirley Chisholm's mother, Ruby, and father, Charles, were part of that migration. Known to each other in Barbados, they reconnected and married in Brooklyn, New York. And that's where they made a home and had Shirley and her two sisters.

Charles and Ruby worked hard to support their family, but money was still tight. The hours were long, and the northern winters were tough for them to get used to. So when Shirley was three years old, her parents sent her and her sisters to Barbados to live with their grandmother. There they could play outside all year round in the warm weather and get a great education. After more than five years, the family reunited. Shirley finished school in Brooklyn, where she was a good student and a natural-born leader. After graduating, she decided to pursue a career in teaching, one of the few professional paths available to black women in the 1940s.

Working as a teacher, Shirley noticed that the school system often failed to provide the teachers, textbooks, and facilities that the students truly needed. It became clear to her that politics and money made the difference between a school that received support and a neglected one. She began to volunteer for political organizations, like the League of Women Voters and her local Democratic club in Brooklyn.

Shirley loved volunteering, and her natural leadership ability was apparent to the women and men she worked with. Many women admired her for her courage and willingness to stand up for herself and speak out on behalf of

> **"If they don't give you a seat at the table, bring a folding chair."**

others. For years, women had been doing much of the behind-the-scenes work for community organizations and political parties, while men took leadership positions and were almost always the candidates running for office. Shirley rejected the notion that women were not meant to lead. Smart, capable, and passionate, she solved problems. She was a leader at work and in her community. So why not serve in government?

First, Shirley ran for and was elected to the New York State Assembly, where she served from 1965 to 1968. Encouraged by her own achievements, she ran for the US House of Representatives and won—a first for a black woman! At the time, there were only 11 women and only 11 black members of the House of Representatives and the Senate. In 1969, Shirley became the one and only black woman in Congress. She arrived in Washington, DC, and hired an all-female staff. She then committed herself to addressing housing inequality, education, and the well-being of children by writing laws and creating programs to help the poor buy food. One of her successful initiatives was the expansion of the Food Stamp program. She said in a speech to fellow legislators, "Our children, our jobless men, our deprived, rejected, and starving fellow citizens, must come first."

Shirley served for seven straight terms in the House of Representatives, retiring in 1982. During this time, she took one big step forward and did something no woman or black man had ever done in politics: she ran for president of the United States as a major party candidate. In 1972, she ran against a field of white men, including then-governor of Alabama George Wallace, who was an admitted white supremacist. Shirley was bold in her statements. "I am not the candidate of black America, although I am black and proud. I am not the candidate of the woman's movement of this country, although

A CONGRESS OF CAUCUSES

Members of the House and the Senate organize themselves into groups in order to better promote their causes. There are hundreds of these groups, or caucuses, in Congress, and the Congressional Black Caucus is among them. The group officially formed in 1971 as a fix for the isolation black elected officials felt, being such a small minority among their colleagues. Shirley Chisolm was one of the 13 founding members. Working together, they knew they could better represent the interests of black Americans.

I am a woman and I am equally proud of that," she said when she announced her candidacy.

Even though Shirley was great at her job and a talented campaigner, she had to deal with a lot of criticism and prejudice. She was criticized by white people because she was a black woman and by black men who believed women were not suited to lead. Shirley said being a woman made her pursuit of politics more difficult than being black. She later observed, "In the end, anti-black, anti-female, and all forms of discrimination are equivalent to the same thing: anti-humanism."

Sexism and racism weren't the only things wrong in American politics. Shirley knew that many people in Congress also participated in unethical practices, such as exchanging money and gifts for votes and influence. So Shirley Chisholm made "Unbossed and Unbought" her campaign slogan to set herself apart as a leader who made decisions based on her principles.

Shirley lost her bid to be the Democratic Party's nominee for president, but that did not diminish her lifetime of great accomplishments. She served as a mentor and teacher for new generations of women and men who were inspired by her to get involved in politics and continue her legacy of social change.

"I want history to remember me not just as the first black woman to be elected to Congress, not as the first black woman to have made a bid for the presidency of the United States, but as a black woman who lived in the twentieth century and dared to be herself. I want to be remembered as a catalyst for change in America."

BESSIE COLEMAN

Bessie Coleman's family was picking cotton in the South to keep a roof overhead and food on the table when she came into the world in 1892. The desire to live a different kind of life bubbled up inside her despite the poverty in which she lived. She chose education as the path to a better life. Doing laundry and picking cotton with her mom in Texas, she saved what little money she made. By the time she was 18 years old, she was able to go to the Colored Agricultural and Normal University (now known as Langston University) in Oklahoma. Her money ran out, though, after only one school term. She was forced to return home to Waxahachie, Texas, for a while.

Four years later, Bessie moved to Chicago to live with two of her brothers. She went to beauty school and found work as a manicurist in the African American barbershops on the city's South Side. The pay was good, and life in the city fueled a fire within her to do big things. After her brothers returned from World War I, they regaled her with stories of their time in Europe. They had been stationed in France, living among people who treated them more as equals and didn't burden them with American-style racist attitudes. What they had to say—especially about the lifestyles of French women—touched a nerve in Bessie. She too wanted to live a life were she could be anything she wanted to be.

The story goes that one day her brother John said, "You [black] women ain't never goin' to fly! Not like those women I saw in France." Well, Bessie was not one to be told—especially by her own brother— what she could and couldn't do. He'd given her the great idea that yes, she most certainly could—with the right instruction—fly a plane. Finding a school that would accept her, a black woman, turned out to be an obstacle until a friend named Robert Abbott, the publisher of the city's

African American newspaper, the *Chicago Defender*, suggested that she go to France to pursue her studies. So she did!

In 1920, Bessie sailed to France and found a flight school that accepted her. She got a break from the racial tensions in the United States and received the training she sought. By the time she returned home a year later, word had spread. A group of reporters were waiting at the harbor to greet her, the black woman licensed to fly a plane.

Even though Bessie had made history by earning her pilot's license, no one in the United States was willing to hire her as a pilot. She was once again struggling to support herself. So she decided to make money by performing tricks in the air. She just had to learn how to do them first! Bessie returned to Europe for more instruction.

This time, after she returned to New York in August 1922, she got right to work. She performed her first air show on September 3, 1922, at Curtiss Field near New York City using a plane borrowed from inventor and aviator Glenn Curtiss. Shows there and in Memphis and Chicago wowed audiences. She took a job flying advertisements in California. Bessie earned enough money then to buy a plane of her own and pursue her larger goal—starting a flight school to teach other African Americans. Soon after purchasing a plane in California, it stalled mid-air and crashed, leaving Bessie injured. She got back in the pilot's seat, but years passed before she could buy another airplane. Bessie held a series of lectures in black theaters in Florida and Georgia to earn money. She even opened a beauty shop in Orlando for a while.

She borrowed planes to continue her exhibition flying and occasional parachute jumping, and she finally managed to buy another plane in April 1926. Sadly, when she and her mechanic took it up for a test flight, it malfunctioned. The mechanic lost control of the plane, and Bessie fell from the open cockpit. She died that day, but what she accomplished in her lifetime paved the way for generations of black people to soar.

Bessie Coleman's dream of a flight school for African Americans was realized in 1929 when William J. Powell established the Bessie Coleman Aero Club in Los Angeles.

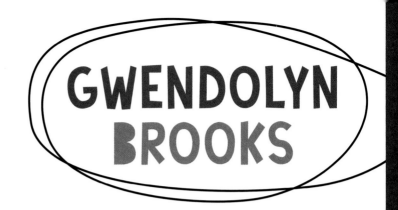

GWENDOLYN BROOKS

"Poetry is life distilled," according to Gwendolyn Brooks. It certainly defined hers. Born in Topeka, Kansas, in 1917, and raised in Chicago, she began writing in her youth. She published her first poem in a journal called *American Childhood* at age 13. Young Gwendolyn was encouraged to create by her mom, a teacher and classically trained pianist, and her father, who supported the family as a janitor. Her mom, Keziah, made a point of taking her to see the great writers of the day, such as Langston Hughes and James Weldon Johnson, when they were in town. At these events, Keziah insisted that 16-year-old Gwen introduce herself to the writers and show her work. Hughes told her she had talent. He said that if she kept writing, she'd be published one day. Sure enough, by the time Gwendolyn was 17, her work regularly appeared in the *Chicago Defender*, a newspaper respected by African Americans across the country.

Her first collection of poetry, *A Street in Bronzeville*, was published in 1945. In it, Gwendolyn portrayed black people in urban settings, often living in "kitchenette buildings," tight spaces where cooking, living, and sleeping were done in one room. Her poems featured characters based on people from her own life, such as nightclub singers living lonely lives and "old-marrieds," who were worn out by their impoverished and crowded city lives.

Gwendolyn wrote about real hardship, but she weaved humor and joyfulness through her work as well. In her writing, she brings readers into the intimate spaces of black neighborhoods: into the beauty parlors and barbershops where hair is dressed for success, into homes where families shared meals and laughter, and out onto the stoops where workers could express how they really felt about their bosses. Her poems were life distilled.

Gwendolyn's poetry touched readers from all walks of life, making her one of America's most beloved and popular writers. She was among the most important voices of the Black Arts Movement in the 1960s and 1970s for her honest and loving portrayal of black America. As Gwendolyn once explained it, "I wrote about what I saw and heard in the street. I lived in a small second-floor apartment at the corner, and I could look first on one side and then on the other. There was my material."

People who don't know much about her otherwise know her widely published poem, "We Real Cool," from *The Bean Eaters*, which includes:

> **We real cool. We**
> **Left school. We**
> **Lurk late.**

She met young people over the years who knew and recited the rhythmic poem, which is both candid about the harsh realities of life in black communities and filled with a spirit that suggests hope and redemption.

Gwendolyn published more than 20 books over the course of her career. Though she worked with some mainstream publishers and black-owned presses, her final publishing home was Third World Press, an independent organization founded by Haki Madhubuti, an activist and poet who regards her as a beloved mentor. "Her greatest lesson to us all," Haki once wrote, "is that serving one's community as an artist means much more than just creating art."

Gwendolyn received a multitude of awards, tributes, and accolades over the course of her life. But her highest honor came when she was just 32 years old. In 1950, she won the Pulitzer Prize for Poetry. She received the award for *Annie Allen*, a collection that revealed the inner life of a young black girl navigating a world that was often hostile to who she was. She was the first black writer to win a Pulitzer Prize.

BROWN GIRL LOVE

Gwendolyn Brooks published only one novel, *Maud Martha*. In it, she portrays a brown-skinned girl growing from adolescence to womanhood, slighted by racially prejudiced white people and "color-struck" black people, who believed that light skin was a ticket to a better life.

FAITH RINGGOLD

As a child, Faith Ringgold was often kept home from school because of her asthma. She passed the time alone by making art. Once she felt better and was back in the company of other children, she still spent her time being creative and making beautiful things. "I was constantly doing art, but I didn't think of myself as an artist. It was just something I liked to do," she said. Faith might have gotten her artsy side from her mother, a fashion designer, who encouraged her daughter to exercise her creativity. Faith also found inspiration in the place where they lived, Harlem, a historic area in New York City known for its African American arts community. Before and during Faith's life, it was the home of composer Duke Ellington, painters Jacob Lawrence and Aaron Douglas, and writer Langston Hughes.

Faith grew up near the City College of New York. She often watched students walk back and forth from campus. But what she didn't notice until she applied to the school herself was that the students were all white and male. Supported by taxpayer dollars, the school was an option for any student who could not afford tuition at a private university. She enrolled but was originally told that she could not major in art because "women did not receive liberal arts degrees." Eventually, the school decided that as long as she also studied education, she could study art. In 1950, the same year she started at City College, she married musician Robert Earl Wallace. The pair had two daughters, Michele Faith and Barbara Faith.

Faith took as many art classes as she could and received a bachelor's degree in fine art and education in 1955. Her job teaching art in public schools helped her pay for her graduate studies in art. She graduated and included her family in her artistic adventures. When she traveled by

AN AUTHOR TOO!

Faith Ringgold is just as famous as a children's book author and illustrator. Published in 1991, her first book, *Tar Beach*, was a Caldecott Honor Book and the winner of the Coretta Scott King Award for illustration, among other awards. It is set on the tar rooftops of buildings where families such as hers went to cool off in the summer. Families and friends came together on roofs to play cards, share meals, and look at the stars. In the book, Faith wrote, "Sleeping on tar beach was magical. Lying on the roof in the night, with stars and skyscraper buildings all around me, made me feel rich, like I owned all that I could see."

ocean liner to look at art in the museums and galleries of Europe in the 1960s, she brought her mother and daughters along. She knew her mother would enjoy the experience and her children would learn and make memories to carry with them for the rest of their lives. Few Americans—especially black women traveling with their family—had the opportunity to travel abroad. Seeing great works of art in person and experiencing French culture opened her eyes to new possibilities for herself.

Early in her career, Faith painted beautiful landscapes. But a gallery owner who was impressed with her talent made her think twice about her flowery subjects. After their meeting, Faith began to look around at what was happening in society as inspiration for her work. There was a lot of political tension in America and around the world in the 1960s, and she decided that she wanted to reflect it in her art. In the late 1960s, Faith did a collection of paintings called *American People*. They were up-close portraits of men and women from all walks of life. When the National Museum of Women in the Arts held an exhibit of the 49 canvases in 2013, they described them as "bold, provocative paintings in direct response to the civil rights and feminist movements." She even showed scenes of riots or portraits of people covered by a bleeding flag. "I wanted to create art that made people stop and *look*," she said.

Faith was a storyteller at heart, and she wrote her family life into stories she created about real people, including historical figures such as Frederick Douglass. She wrote scripts for live performances and made paintings, some on pieces of fabric stitched together to make the image whole. She also created soft sculptures, masks, and dolls depicting influential people such as President Jimmy Carter and his family.

In the early 1980s, she began to make story quilts using both text and bold images. These quilts showed the suffering and joy, and the losses and victories of black people—and they became her most popular type of work. Her first story quilt, *Who's Afraid of Aunt Jemima?*, uses words and images to break down the stereotype of black women as maids who only have worth when they are laboring for others. Faith wanted to provoke her audience. She said, "You've got to get 'em and hold 'em. The more they look, the more they see." In the late 1990s, she depicted the Statue of Liberty as a black woman and created a scene of historical figures Frederick Douglass, Harriet Tubman (see page 36), and Sojourner Truth together in conversation. In sharing her vision of the world, Faith not only became a world-class artist but also a feminist icon and a leading voice for black people in America.

Her work has been shown in museums and galleries around the world, and she has received many grants, fellowships, and prestigious awards, including 23 honorary doctorates. Her public commissions, like those of Xenobia Bailey (see page 58), who followed her, include mosaic murals in subway stations. In the Civic Center/Grand Park subway station in Los Angeles, her *People Portraits* installation includes 52 glass mosaics. The mosaic she designed for New York City's 125th Street subway station, called *Flying Home: Harlem Heroes and Heroines*, features images of black artists, athletes, and leaders, like Josephine Baker, Zora Neale Hurston (see page 106), Jesse Owens, Sugar Ray Robinson, and Malcolm X.

Faith created artwork to express her feelings about people's inhumanity to one another, exploring subjects from American slavery to the bombing of the World Trade Center on September 11, 2001. "Out of every awful thing is something beautiful," Faith has said. "As an artist, I want to see beauty."

"I CAN'T TELL YOUR STORY, I CAN ONLY TELL MINE. I CAN'T BE YOU, I CAN ONLY BE ME."

MICHELLE OBAMA

Michelle LaVaughn Robinson grew up the daughter of a city water worker and a former secretary in a small second-floor apartment in a house on the South Side of Chicago. She and her brother, Craig, were raised with the expectation that they would pursue a higher education and join a profession. And they did. When Michelle graduated from high school, she followed her brother to Princeton University. After graduating, she went her own way, earning her law degree from Harvard Law School in 1988. Soon after passing the bar exam (the test lawyers take in order to practice law), she landed a job back in Chicago, at a firm called Sidley & Austin (now Sidley Austin LLP). Michelle was working as a marketing and intellectual property lawyer when she was assigned to mentor an intern at the firm. His name was Barack Obama.

The pair were married in 1992. By then, Michelle had left corporate law behind and begun a career in public service. Like her father, Michelle worked for the City of Chicago. First, she served as an assistant to Mayor Richard Daley, and then she became the assistant commissioner of planning and development, a government agency that deals with all sorts of issues, like encouraging the development of new businesses, ensuring that neighborhoods are walkable and waterfront areas are accessible, and providing assistance to renters and first-time home buyers. In 1993, she became the first executive director of the Chicago office of Public Allies, a program that helps young people train for careers in public service. Three years later, Michelle began working at the University of Chicago, eventually ending up as vice president of community and external affairs for the University of Chicago Medical Center in 2005. The prestigious university's campus was close to the home she'd grown up in—but back then it seemed like it was worlds away.

On November 4, 2008, Michelle's life and career changed forever. In a stunning victory, Barack Obama became the first African American president of the United States, and Michelle LaVaughn Robinson Obama became the nation's first African American First Lady. While Michelle initially resisted the public life of presidential politics, she took her partnership with the president and her service to her country seriously and set out to redefine the role of First Lady.

She declared herself mom-in-chief as a statement of her commitment to her two daughters—but the title also matched well with the kinds of programs she initiated on behalf of all American families. Her office in the White House created programs to make healthy living easier and education more accessible to all. In 2009, Michelle worked with her team and a group of local elementary school children to plant a vegetable garden on the White House lawn. She wanted to keep her family healthy and promote the importance of cooking at home and eating fresh produce. In a speech, she said, "This is a passion. . . . I am determined to work with folks across this country to change the way a generation of kids thinks about food and nutrition."

One of her most ambitious goals was to end childhood obesity within a generation. So, in 2010, Michelle launched a program called Let's Move! to encourage children and adults to eat healthy foods and be active—to dance, work out, play sports, and get fit. She helped pass the Healthy, Hunger-Free Kids Act of 2010, a bill that provided nutritional free and reduced-price lunches to more than 21 million low-income children. Michelle was also committed to improving the lives of military families.

"If there's one thing I've learned in life, it's the power of using your voice."

As First Lady, she had her detractors, as did President Obama. But Michelle kept her poise when confronted with haters. As she said in a famous speech at the 2016 Democratic National Convention, "When they go low, we go high." Her memoir, *Becoming*, was the best-selling book of 2018. Her good works, grace, warmth, and style have made her one of the most popular and beloved women in the world.

GLORY EDIM

Glory Edim has been a well-read black girl for as long as she can remember. Her mother began teaching her to read years before she went to regular school. And Glory and her brothers went to the public library most days of the week. That's where they did their homework, and where they explored, wrote stories, and made up plays. She credits libraries for teaching her about community building—for cultivating a "sense of belonging and understanding that things could be shared in a way that built more than just community, but kinship and family."

Both of Glory's parents were born in Nigeria, but they spent most of their married life in Arlington, Virginia. After her parents divorced when Glory was in the sixth grade, her dad returned to Africa, where Glory would visit in the summer. Divorce is hard on everyone in a family, and Glory's experience was no different. She learned to navigate her ups and downs, in part by digging in to good books.

While Glory was in college, her mother was not in good health. Unable to lean on her mother or heal her, Glory found comfort in the works of great black writers. In her mind, she walked in the shoes of the characters these writers created and found herself feeling nourished and revived. After she finished her studies at Howard University and went out into the working world, she missed the moral support and encouragement she had enjoyed at an HBCU. Glory turned to literature to lift her up when the corporate work world wore her down. She has said in interviews that women writers, such as Toni Cade Bambara, bell hooks, and Audre Lorde "helped shape [her] own sense of self-worth."

Reading became so much a part of her daily practice that her longtime boyfriend surprised her with a gift: a custom T-shirt printed with a list of her favorite authors and the nickname: "Well-Read Black Girl."

Every time Glory wore it—in the gym, around her Brooklyn neighborhood, anywhere—it sparked conversation with others about how much they loved those authors too.

> "Everyone deserves to have their stories told and held with integrity and dignity."

It occurred to Glory that people were hungry for more than just reading books they could relate to. She realized that people also wanted to talk with others about what they read. So, in 2015, she launched the Well-Read Black Girl Instagram account to build a community of like-minded people. It took off so well that she decided to host an in-person book discussion around a single title. For the first meeting, the group read *Between the World and Me*, by Ta-Nehisi Coates. The first gathering of the Well-Read Black Girl Book Club drew a small but enthusiastic group. Next, she picked *The Star Side of Bird Hill*. This debut novel, by Naomi Jackson, was taking the literary community by storm—and Naomi was there in person to join the discussion. Glory particularly likes to promote great writers who are at the beginning of their career. The established writers, she has said, "are the foundation, but what does the next generation look like? How can we uplift that?"

For the next two books, Glory chose a novel by Angela Flournoy and a memoir by Pulitzer Prize–winner Margo Jefferson. The regulars attending the book club grew to 30 or more people. Glory's brand was on the rise, and she grew it even more when she put readers and writers in the same room. In November 2017, she hosted the first annual Well-Read Black Girl Festival. The event drew 300 people, who came to see A-list authors, including Jacqueline Woodson, Renée Watson, Nic Stone, and Tayari Jones. By the end of 2019, the group's social media following blew up to nearly 350,000 followers.

Glory created a space where black women readers can come together with each other and with brilliant writers whose work has sometimes changed their lives. In the process, she has become a recognized leader in the literary world. She has also edited a collection of essays and interviews herself. *Well-Read Black Girl: Finding Our Stories, Discovering Ourselves* came out in October 2018.

ABBEY LINCOLN

Abbey Lincoln was born Anna Marie Wooldridge to a big family in Chicago in 1930, during the Great Depression. This national economic crisis left people struggling to meet basic needs. Abbey's parents were industrious and resilient people, but the family didn't have much. Her father built the house they lived in. And later, he built the family a home near Kalamazoo, Michigan, where they moved when Abbey was a small child. "There was a piano in the house," she recalled, "and when I was near to five years of age, I started to experiment with the piano because there were so many people in the house. We didn't have any privacy, but I could find that at the piano—privacy and some serenity." No matter where the family lived, music—and a piano—were ever present.

As a teen, Abbey sang in her school's band. When she was 20, her brother took her to California, where she eventually began to sing in nightclubs in San Diego. She then found an agent, who sent her to perform in Hawaii. The gorgeous Pacific island had military bases and a vibrant club scene that kept soldiers and their families entertained and talented young singers employed. When she returned to California two years later, she began performing at clubs like the Moulin Rouge in Los

> **"I gravitate to songs that help me to live— because if you sing something over and over, you say something over and over, and if you set it to music, it really is a prayer. It goes up into the atmosphere, and it will bring you the return of what you've been saying."**

Angeles. She wore elegant long gowns and used a stage name, Gaby Wooldridge. Later, she went by Gabby Lee. "I was becoming a glamorous woman," she recalled.

She was making a living on her own with her music, but she wanted more. Abbey found that she needed someone to help her book new gigs, build her profile, and manage her money. She soon found herself a manager, and one of the things he suggested was that she choose a better stage name. About her potential new last name, she recalled him grinning and saying to her, "Since Abraham Lincoln didn't free the slaves, maybe you can handle it." She agreed to the name change and made her first recording—with the saxophonist and band leader Benny Carter—as Abbey Lincoln.

The music of the 1950s is remembered for the many talented African Americans who played jazz, which some people consider America's only original art form. Abbey absorbed and built on the traditions of musicians who came before her. "I sing in the tradition of Billie Holliday, Sarah Vaughn, Dinah Washington, and Ella Fitzgerald," Abbey said. She grew up listening to these artists, who were great storytellers. They provided her with the foundation for creating her own original music. "I just sing about my life," she explained. Abbey wrote a song called "Throw It Away" after reading the *I Ching*, a book used as a tool to divine the future and to gain self-insight. One of the book's messages is that you can't lose in life what is rightfully yours.

Abbey brought passion and depth to her music, including the songs "The People in Me" and "A Circle of Love," which are about the connection people have to each other across nationality, race, and ethnicity, and the possibility of peace and harmony among humans. She also wrote personal songs, like a tribute to her father and a tribute to her mother. Her work, including beloved songs like "The World Is Falling

REVOLUTION AS ART

Abbey Lincoln recorded *We Insist!: Max Roach's Freedom Now Suite*, written by Max Roach and singer/songwriter Oscar Brown Jr. The album told the story of the African American experience, the triumphs and tragedies. Released in 1960, it is one of the most famous jazz albums ever recorded, not only because the music was innovative, but also because it demonstrated the power of art.

Down," "The Music Is the Magic," and so many others, came from a spiritual, honest, loving place.

During her marriage to percussionist Max Roach and for a brief period afterward, Abbey stepped away from recording. In 1972, two years after their divorce, she traveled to Africa, an inevitable part of her journey. There, she was met with respect, as a descendant, an artist, and an activist. While visiting Guinea and Zaire (now the Democratic Republic of the Congo), she was even given two new names, which she combined into one, Aminata Moseka, and treasured for the rest of her life. After her return to the United States, Abbey was back in the studio full force, beginning with her 1973 release, *People in Me*.

Abbey believed in the power of art to carry a moving message and affirm people's humanity. She especially believed in the artistic genius found in black people. And she understood the power of images to build up or break down people's spirits, so she chose to wear an afro in an era when black women were made to feel ashamed about their hair. "I felt beautiful and whole when I started to wear my hair natural," she has said. Abbey was regarded by many as a great beauty. She appeared on the cover of magazines, but said, "I wasn't raised to believe that being what you looked like was supposed to mean anything." She explained, "Mama always taught us that pretty is as pretty does."

●N THE ●IG SCREEN

Abbey's work as an actress is as celebrated as her work as a musician. She was the leading lady in the 1964 film *Nothing But a Man* and, a few years later, she starred in *For Love of Ivy* alongside Sidney Poitier, then the biggest black star in Hollywood. Both films remain critically acclaimed classics. In 1993, she said in an interview, "More people know my work as an actress than they do as a singer. . . . It's been hard for the people in the [entertainment] industry to keep up with me and to figure out what it is I really am. Because I've had all these names and all these different careers."

SHONDA RHIMES

Shonda Rhimes is a living example of what happens when intention and preparation meet opportunity. She was a shy child, she says. The youngest of six siblings, she would hide in the kitchen pantry and use canned food as the actors and props in the stories she imagined. Her mother didn't mind. She wanted all of her children to use their imaginations and be creative.

Shonda prepared herself with a good education. While attending Dartmouth College, she wrote fiction as well as articles for the campus paper. She also acted and directed for a group called the Black Underground Theater Association. She graduated in 1991. While deciding what to do next, she read an article that said it was harder to get into the University of Southern California's (USC) film school than it was to get into Harvard Law School. Naturally competitive, she applied. And, three years later, she earned a master of fine arts degree (MFA).

While at USC, Shonda worked as an intern for Hollywood producer Debra Martin Chase, who became her mentor. Debra helped her get her first jobs in the industry, including a position as the research director for a documentary on baseball player Hank Aaron. Then, in 1998, Shonda wrote and directed her own short film called *Blossoms and Veils*. The independent film didn't have the backing of a big production company that could get it shown in theaters across the nation. But it did have a cast that included big stars like Jeffrey Wright and Jada Pinkett Smith.

Also in 1998, she landed the job as co-writer of a 1999 TV movie called *Introducing Dorothy Dandridge*, starring Halle Berry. Shonda's biggest job to date, it told the story of one of black America's first big movie stars. Next up, she was hired to write the 2002 film *Crossroads*, starring Britney Spears. And Debra continued to help her protégée. When

she produced *The Princess Diaries 2*, she brought Shonda in as a writer. Working on a big studio film like that opened new doors for Shonda.

As a screenwriter, she aimed "to write people I wanted to watch." Her stories would defy stereotypes. And beyond that, she wanted to write characters that would show the full range of what people do in life and how they behave. In an interview with Oprah Winfrey (see page 118), she said, "Most of the women I saw on TV didn't seem like people I actually knew. They felt like ideas of what women are. They never got to be nasty or competitive or hungry or angry. They were often just the loving wife or the nice friend. . . . Who gets to be the three-dimensional woman?" When Shonda couldn't find complex women on TV, she created them.

What happened next would make her one of the rare writers who becomes a power player inside the industry and a household name at the same time. In less than 10 years, she created not one but three blockbuster shows on network television: *Grey's Anatomy* (2005), *Private Practice* (2007), and *Scandal* (2012). These shows drew huge audiences and become enormous hits. They featured diverse casts, including black and Asian characters and women who were strong, accomplished, and flawed in all the ways that real people are. Shonda is the first woman to have three hit television shows, each with more than 100 episodes. In addition to creating the shows, she also served as a showrunner. Showrunners are in charge of just about everything on a show and make final decisions on creative, financial, and management issues.

By being inclusive and daring in her representations of characters, especially women, this queen of prime-time television has changed the face of entertainment. In 2018, she was the highest-paid showrunner in Hollywood. "Dreams do not come true just because you dream them," Shonda said. "It's hard work that makes things happen. It's hard work that creates change."

LEARNING TO SAY "YES"

In 2015, Shonda Rhimes published a book. Entitled *A Year of Yes: How to Dance It Out, Stand in the Sun, and Be Your Own Person*, it tells the story of how she overcame her shyness and learned how to be more open to new experiences and opportunities.

SHIRLEY ANN JACKSON

As a child in Washington, DC, Shirley Ann Jackson's idea of a good time was playing with bumblebees in her backyard. She'd catch them and put them in a mason jar with holes punched in the lid so the bees could breathe. That way, she could study what they ate and how they acted. An inquisitive girl, she wanted to know what made wasps different from yellow jackets and bumblebees different from honeybees.

Shirley wanted to become a scientist, and she was cheered on by supportive adults at home and at school. When it was time for her to go to college, one administrator encouraged her to apply to the Massachusetts Institute of Technology (MIT). It was the school of choice for students pursuing careers in science and engineering. It was not known for admitting many women or African Americans, but otherwise it was perfect.

Shirley joined the MIT class of 1968. The coursework was challenging, but for her, the hard part was fitting in with her fellow students and teachers. Once, when she attempted to join a study group in her dormitory, the group told her to "go away." It wasn't their help that Shirley needed—she knew how to solve the homework problems—it was their company she sought. Her feelings were hurt, but all she could do was collect her books and return to her room.

Shirley didn't wallow in her hurt feelings, though, and she kept moving forward and even devoted herself to helping others. She volunteered in a hospital ward, caring for babies and young children. It was the height of the civil rights movement. Racial tensions came to a boiling point in April 1968 when Martin Luther King Jr. was assassinated. It was a turning point in history—and a turning point in Shirley's life. She said, "I had been a pretty quiet student before then, focusing on what I was doing: my work, physics, working in the lab." But now she was

motivated to become more politically active. She got together with the few other African American students on campus and organized what would become a black student union. Together they presented some demands to the campus leadership and asked that they make some changes. They spoke to the school's administrators and proposed ways to attract more black students to MIT and to improve the quality of their college experience once they came. Their activism paid off. The university formed a Task Force on Educational Opportunity and took other steps to make life on their campus better for students of color. She stayed at MIT and got her PhD in physics in 1973.

By the time Shirley left MIT, she had made history as the first African American woman to receive a PhD at the school. After getting her doctorate, she went on to conduct research at AT&T Bell Laboratories and hold important positions on a US Department of Energy task force and the New Jersey Commission on Science and Technology. She began teaching classes at Rutgers University in the early 1990s. And, in 1995, President Bill Clinton appointed her chair of the US Nuclear Regulatory Commission. Four years later, she became the president of Rensselaer Polytechnic Institute.

Shirley Ann Jackson may not be a household name, but her work has touched the lives of the masses. Her research has been used in the technology that improves phones and cables, making person-to-person communication more reliable. And her research has helped pave the way for the kinds of supercomputers that will exist in the future. But what might be more exciting is her work to help eliminate our dependence on fossil fuels. She was part of the team whose research helped create better solar cells, which take the sun's energy and turns it into electricity.

In 2016, she received the nation's highest science honor. President Barack Obama presented Shirley with the National Medal of Science "for her insightful work in condensed matter physics and particle physics, for her science-rooted public policy achievements, and for her inspiration to the next generation of professionals in the science, technology, engineering, and math fields."

"Never let others define what your life can be."

SIMONE BILES

It is no wonder interviewers ask Simone Biles if she is real. As a champion gymnast, she appears superhuman, making jaw-dropping tumbling passes and exceptional dismounts from the balance beam. She is an extraordinary athlete, but she is also a fabulous and regular girl who has had more than her share of obstacles to overcome.

Born in 1997 in Columbus, Ohio, she and her three siblings were put into foster care because her parents suffered from substance abuse and addiction. Luckily they had family who could help. Their grandfather and step-grandmother brought Simone and her sister Adria—the youngest of the siblings—to live with them in Spring, Texas. (They are the ones Simone calls *dad* and *mom*.) And Simone's great-aunt took responsibility for her two older siblings. Although the children ended up in different homes, they remained with family members and had stable and loving upbringings.

Simone was very young when she was in foster care. She doesn't remember a lot about the experience, but she does talk freely to the media about the hardship of her early years because, in her words, "it's important for kids to know that you don't have to grow up in certain environments to make something good [of your life]. I was in a foster home and now, I'm an Olympic gymnast."

When she was six years old, Simone saw children doing gymnastics while on a day-care field trip. She immediately began mimicking what she saw and asking her parents about taking lessons. Soon after, she started training at Bannon's Gymnastix in Houston, Texas. She made the decision to pursue her sport professionally in the eighth grade. It meant that she'd have to leave public school and be homeschooled. She was sad that she wouldn't be around her friends as much. But, after a talk with her mom, she realized that her "friends will always still be there." She understood

that pursuing her dream of being a top-tier athlete meant developing her skills *now*. In her autobiography, *Courage to Soar*, Simone wrote that starting gymnastics at age six was "actually pretty late for an elite gymnast. Most girls are flipping and tumbling in mommy and me classes before they're three, so in a way, I'd been playing catch-up. But if there's one thing everyone knows about me, it's that I love a challenge."

Although Simone was a little older than most when she started training, she was smaller than her fellow gymnasts. By age 14, she was only 4 feet, 8 inches tall. She was stronger than most, though. She wrote, "I'd been born with the kind of biceps and muscled calves that, back in third grade, had earned me the nickname *swoldger*—a cross between *swollen* and *soldier*." She didn't like it at first. "But after a while," she wrote, "I embraced it. I was like, *Yeah, I'm stronger than half of the boys in my class, so don't mess with me.*"

> **"I feel like you should never settle just because you're winning or you're at the top. You should always push yourself."**

Simone wasn't always confident and secure, and she didn't always perform well. She is, after all, human. She missed making the national team in 2011 by one spot. At the US Classic in 2013, she said, "I fell almost on every event. . . . It was really bad." For a while, she was hesitant to see a sports psychologist. But she did, and she learned a lot. She realized that she was worrying about what other people thought of her. Other people's comments were affecting her—especially when they talked about her body. She knew she was fit, but she overheard a coach at the US Classic describe her as fat and blame her poor performance on that. Her parents, her coaches, and her therapist helped her work through it all—just in time to give a powerhouse performance at the 2013 US National Championship competition.

In 2014, Simone became the first woman in 40 years to win four gold medals at a single World Championship—a feat she repeated in 2015 and 2018. The US Olympic Committee named her Female Olympic Athlete of the Year in 2015. The following year, she was the Associated Press Female Athlete of the Year.

With great success, Simone also felt great pressure. Early in 2016, as she prepared for the Olympics, she said, "I swore I lost every skill I had ever done. . . . I freaked out a little bit because I was nervous." At 19 years old, she was feeling unsure of herself. But she was nowhere close to giving up. She dug in and worked through the rough patch with the help of her teammates. She did "so many repetitions and sets" until she and her team "were so confident, not only in ourselves but in each other, so once we went out there it was just like okay, when we're a team, we can do this." Their dedication paid off. At the Olympic Games in Rio de Janeiro, Simone won five medals—four gold, one bronze.

Simone found success outside of the gym as well with her memoir. After the book came out, she took a break from training to promote it and spend time with family and friends—and travel the world. She went to Hawaii, Belize, England, and Monaco, among other places. A year or so later, in her words, she "started slowing everything down and then decided to get back into the gym."

Before long, the 22-year-old was back in action and breaking her own records. At the 2019 National Championships, Simone pulled off an astonishing double-double dismount on the balance beam—that's a double twist, double flip combo—that no one but her has ever landed in competition. Later that weekend, she accomplished another first: she became the first woman to complete a triple-double in her floor routine— three full twists and two flips. By the end of the competition, she had won her sixth US Gymnastics Championships title. Now Simone is tied with gymnast Clara Schroth-Lomady (who competed in the 1940s and 1950s) for winning the most all-around national titles in the United States.

Simone is still making superhuman accomplishments in her field and continuing to write her own story. Some might say it's about how a short, curvy girl became the GOAT (greatest of all time) in her sport. But, Simone says it's about "how my faith and my family made my wildest dreams come true. And how embracing a dream can give you courage to soar."

Simone's father built her a gym in Spring, Texas. Known as "the Centre," it's 52,000 square feet with 40-foot-high ceilings, a giant foam pit, and signs that say "no parents allowed."

ELLA BAKER

Before Ella Baker dedicated her life to the fight for civil rights, she was a curious child in North Carolina who learned about enslavement from a woman who lived it: her grandmother. Ella has recalled her grandmother telling her about the brutality of enslavement and the punishment she received for rebelling against slave owners. Perhaps Ella learned to stand up for herself by listening to her grandmother's tales. And perhaps hearing the truth about how her own grandmother had been mistreated inspired her to fight injustice whenever she saw it from then on.

After the turn of the twentieth century, African Americans had more options than ever before for how they wanted to work and live. In Ella's case, she chose to pursue a college education at Shaw University in Raleigh, North Carolina. She had the intelligence and drive to do well in her courses and, in 1927, she was the valedictorian of her graduating class. While at Shaw, she also challenged the administration when she believed school policies to be unfair. Her student activism was a warm-up to the political activism that she would soon be known for.

After college, Ella moved to Harlem and joined the forefront of activism. She actively participated in organizations that addressed the economic and labor issues of minorities, including people of color and women. She became committed to the belief that "people cannot be free until there is enough work in

THE HARLEM RENAISSANCE

There was a great burst of accomplishments in education, the arts, and society in the 1910s, 1920s, and 1930s in New York City. Professor Alain Locke called this creative explosion the New Negro movement. The uptown neighborhood of Harlem emerged as the capital of this rebirth of black culture, and the period became known as the Harlem Renaissance. Ella Baker thrived in Harlem during this exciting time.

this land to give everybody a job." In 1941, she landed a full-time job with one of the most important civil rights organizations in the country: the National Association for the Advancement of Colored People (NAACP).

As an assistant field secretary for the NAACP, Ella helped advance the organization's goals by supporting existing offices across the country and by creating new branches. In the process, she gained a reputation as a superb strategist, a critical thinker, and a talented organizer—"for a woman," that is. The mostly male leadership of the movement was used to women being in the rank and file but not in leadership positions. And they were not interested in changing their views. Though the NAACP decision makers were men, including many pastors, Ella did not defer to them. When she had an opinion, she expressed it. And, when something needed to be done, she took care of it. "As far as I'm concerned," Ella has said, "I was never working for an organization. I have always tried to work for a cause, and the cause to me is bigger than any organization—bigger than any group of people, and it is the cause of humanity. The cause is the cause that brings us together—the drive of the human spirit for freedom."

Ella continued to participate in voter registration and other campaigns with the NAACP even after she resigned as its director of branches in 1946. She returned to New York City to take care of a family member in need. While there, she found time to work with the local NAACP branch and other organizations on the issue of school integration.

In the mid-1950s, inspired by how the Montgomery Bus Boycott had galvanized black and white people to push against racist segregation, Ella set up an organization to raise money to fight racist laws in the South. Next she was called to Atlanta to work with Stanley Levison, Bayard Rustin, and other civil rights leaders to set up

THE LEADER IS YOU

Ella Baker believed in the ability of young people to lead self-determined lives and not put their fate in the hands of a single or a few charismatic leaders. Ella clashed with some other civil rights leaders over this approach. But she was a persuasive and dedicated grassroots organizer who had a huge impact on the civil rights movement. She asked young people to envision who they wanted to be and what they wanted most in their lives. And she encouraged them to get involved and do what they needed to do in pursuit of those goals.

THE MONTGOMERY BUS BOYCOTT

The Montgomery Improvement Association (MIA), led by Martin Luther King Jr. and Ralph David Abernathy, initiated a boycott in 1955 that forced the bus system in Montgomery, Alabama, to end their racially segregated seating practices. The campaign garnered mass support and captured the attention of media and people around the world. Rosa Parks, the face of the boycott, attended workshops led by Ella Baker as part of her preparation for the protest.

the office of the Southern Christian Leadership Conference (SCLC). With SCLC, Ella organized a voter registration campaign called Crusade for Citizenship in 1958. Over the next two and a half years, she identified and trained workers, organized campaigns for protests, and planned events, including trips around the country to expand support for SCLC.

Ella encouraged Martin Luther King Jr., as the head of SCLC, to bring more women and young people into the organization to better represent the black community. The energy the student activists brought to group actions, such as marches and demonstrations, was making a positive difference, and the older generation of activists who led SCLC started to take notice. Ella understood, in her words, that "the Negro and white students, North and South, are seeking to rid America of the scourge of racial segregation and discrimination—not only at lunch counters, but in every aspect of life." She took a position in support of the youth leaders that, instead of becoming an arm of SCLC, they should have an organization of their own. So Ella worked with these young activists to create the Student Nonviolent Coordinating Committee (SNCC, pronounced *snick*).

Ella strongly believed in the value of the young founders of SNCC. And they respected her for her leadership and experience. Together, they helped make SNCC one of the most influential organizations of the civil rights era. Ella's tireless work earned her the nickname *Fundi*, a Swahili word that refers to an expert who teaches a craft or passes knowledge on to a new generation. She passed away on her 83rd birthday, but her legacy will last forever.

> "No one is going to do for you that which you yourself are unwilling to do."

RESOURCES

BOOKS

Autobiographies

Courage to Soar: A Body in Motion, A Life in Balance by Simone Biles, with Michelle Burford (Zondervan, 2016)

Life in Motion: An Unlikely Ballerina, Young Readers Edition by Misty Copeland, with Brandy Colbert (Aladdin, 2016)

Mo'ne Davis: Remember My Name: My Story from First Pitch to Game Changer by Mo'ne Davis, with Hilary Beard (HarperCollins, 2015)

Select Books by Women in This Book

A Raisin in the Sun by Lorraine Hansberry (Vintage, 2004)

Bronzeville Boys and Girls by Gwendolyn Brooks, illustrated by Faith Ringgold (HarperCollins, 2006)

If a Bus Could Talk: The Story of Rosa Parks by Faith Ringgold (Simon & Schuster Books for Young Readers, 1999)

My Dream of Martin Luther King by Faith Ringgold (Dragonfly Books, 1998)

Sugar Plum Ballerinas (series) by Whoopi Goldberg, with Deborah Underwood, illustrated by Maryn Roos (Disney/Jump at the Sun Books, 2008)

Tar Beach by Faith Ringgold (Knopf Books for Young Readers, 1991)

Their Eyes Were Watching God by Zora Neale Hurston (Amistad, 2016)

Books about Women Featured in This Book

Discovering History's Heroes: Ida B. Wells by Diane Bailey (Aladdin, 2019)

Exquisite: The Poetry and Life of Gwendolyn Brooks by Suzanne Slade, illustrated by Cozbi A. Cabrera (Abrams Books for Young Readers, 2020)

Fearless Mary: Mary Fields, American Stagecoach Driver by Tami Charles, illustrated by Claire Almon (Albert Whitman & Company, 2019)

Harriet Tubman: Conductor on the Underground Railroad by Ann Petry (Amistad, 2018)

Madam C.J. Walker Builds a Business by Rebel Girls, illustrated by Salini Perera (Rebel Girls, 2019)

Who Are Venus and Serena Williams? by James Buckley Jr., illustrated by Andrew Thomson (Penguin Workshop, 2017)

Who Is Michelle Obama? by Megan Stine, illustrated by John O'Brien (Penguin Workshop, 2013)

Who Was Coretta Scott King? by Gail Herman, illustrated by Gregory Copeland (Penguin Workshop, 2017)

Work It, Girl: Blast Off into Space Like Mae Jemison by Caroline Moss, illustrated by Sinem Erkas (Frances Lincoln Children's Books, 2020)

Work It, Girl: Run the Show Like CEO Oprah Winfrey by Caroline Moss, illustrated by Sinem Erkas (Frances Lincoln Children's Books, 2019)

Anthologies of Black Trailblazers

Let It Shine: Stories of Black Women Freedom Fighters by Andrea Davis Pinkney, illustrated by Stephen Alcorn (HMH Books for Young Readers, 2013)

Little Leaders: Bold Women in Black History by Vashti Harrison (Little, Brown Books for Young Readers, 2017)

Young, Gifted and Black: Meet 52 Black Heroes from Past and Present by Jamia Wilson, illustrated by Andrea Pippins (Wide-Eyed Editions, 2018)

WEBSITES

1000 Black Girl Books Resource Guide
grassrootscommunityfoundation.org/1000 -black-girl-books-resource-guide

African American Literature Book Club
aalbc.com

Look online for TED Talks by Stacey Abrams, Debbie Allen, Misty Copeland, Mae Jemison, Michelle Obama, Shonda Rhimes, and Serena Williams

PODCASTS

Flyest Fables

Freedom's Promise

Oprah's SuperSoul Conversations